Everything You Need Is Right Here

Five Steps to Manifesting Magic and Miracles

Avalon Emerging Press
St. Louis, Missouri

Kimberly V. Schneider, M.Ed., J.D., LPC,
The Manifestation Maven

KimberlySchneider.com

Limits of Liability/Disclaimer of Warranty

Reproduction

What People Are Saying About Kimberly Schneider and *Everything You Need Is Right Here*

"...one of the rare, skillful books that actually delivers what it promises. All the wisdom for embracing a life fully animate and thriving, open to the spiritual in the widest sense, is beautifully articulated here. As I browsed through this book initially, the words of two other geniuses of writing came to mind: one, a second century Christian saint, Ireneus; the other, a twenty-first century philosopher and poet, **John O'Donohue**...Kimberly's inspiring poems woven into her marvelous manual lie naturally and easily beside the words of **Jalaluddin Rumi, Meister Eckhart** and **Mahatma Gandhi**, making *Everything You Need Is Right Here* a treasure trove of artistic creativity as well as a cornucopia of right living."

-**Noirin Ni Riain**, author of *Theosony: Towards a Theology of Listening* and *Listen with the Ear of the Heart*

"Since most of our creative power comes from the unconscious, exposing and dismantling deep-seated and limiting beliefs are the real Secret to manifesting. The way Kimberly Schneider demonstrates this in her book only comes from experience. An absolute must for anyone seeking higher consciousness by breaking the psychological and social bonds that hold us back."

- **Rahasya Poe**, author of *To Believe or Not To Believe: The Social and Neurological Consequences of Belief Systems*

"If you find yourself standing bewildered at the gates to conscious manifestation, Kimberly takes you by the hand and guides you every step of the way. By the end of this book, you'll be a Master Conscious Manifester."

-**Peter Beamish**, creator of *Introducing Abraham: The Secret behind The Secret* (DVD), aura.ca

"An informative look at the science and the spirituality of creating positive change and bringing what you want into your life. Its message is want what you will and will what you want. This book shows you how."
- **Ross Heaven**, author of *The Hummingbird's Journey to God* and *The Sin Eater's Last Confessions*

"Some authors teach, others entertain while still others stir your emotions and move you to the very depths of your soul. Kimberly Schneider's book does all this and much more. I could not put it down, not only was it fun to read but also extremely profound. Filled with wisdom and encouragement with a blueprint for a happy, prosperous, productive life even while facing difficulties. I highly recommend it."
- **Don Smith**, founder of VillageEmpowerment.org

"*Everything You Need Is Right Here* is a triptych to a new world . . . a world each reader will be inspired to create for themselves, and guided in just how to do it. Kim Schneider is an empowered, masterful teacher and guide, sharing both lived experience and living wisdom. Each chapter is like a cairn of well-balanced stones of insight and example, each principle and provision carefully placed to support the next, and the next. In recent times, we have been reminded that wherever we go, there we are. *Everything You Need Is Right Here* reminds us of not only what to do once we get there, but how to enjoy the journey as well."
- **Daniel Ansara Page**, Master Astrologer, author of *Lessons in Astrology: The Chart of 2012* (DVD), AnsaraAstrology.com

"A wonderfully accessible 'how to' handbook to manifestation! Full of heartwarming stories from the life of an exceptionally gifted woman generously sharing what she deeply knows heart-to-heart."
- **Emma Bragdon,** Ph.D., author of books about spiritual healing in Brazil: *Kardec's Spiritism: A Home for Healing and Spiritual Evolution* and *Spiritual Alliances: Discovering the Roots of Health at the Casa de Dom Inacio*

"You've read books on manifestation? You've been told to 'think positively' and all your dreams will come true? And yet…you still can't seem to grasp how to really and truly create your life consciously and purposefully and joyfully? Well, Kimberly's book will (really) show you how. Once you've glimpsed her Manifestation Matrix, you'll breathe a sigh of relief at how simple and elegant it all really is. Using candid and authentic glimpses into her own and her family's personal journey, Kimberly takes us right to the heart of what it means to create our own reality. You'll want to read it more than once as you grow into the knowledge of what is your absolute birthright, but perhaps you've forgotten. You are a powerful creator. Read this book and put your power to work for you joyfully and easily. *Everything You Need is Right Here*. And so it is."

   - **Jody Baron**, author of *Relax Into Sex: The Art of Spiritual Lovemaking*

"'*Everything you need to know about how to create the life you want is written in the message of your life*.' Kimberly Schneider's self-revealing book not only invites us into the depths of who she is, it also offers a formidable formula for decoding *your* veiled message. Kimberly's pure intention to facilitate evolution of consciousness positions her perfectly to trigger deep, internal movement in people. If you are truly ready to evolve, let Kimberly's jewel in the cornucopia of life light your way. You won't want to miss this journey!"

   - **Dr. Samantha St. Julian**, Creator of Synergia Healing Arts, Synergia.bz

"Kimberly Schneider is true to her words; she lives what she teaches in this book. While manifestation seems to be a common topic, Kim adds a dimension and perspective that is not clearly taught anywhere else. She teaches how to weave conscious manifestation with Divine surrender in a simple but profound manner that anyone can use. Her teachings reflect her true-life experiences of challenge and triumph that will touch your heart. Reading and studying *Everything You Need Is Right Here* offers honest change to the life of anyone who is willing."

   - **Marilyn Eagen**, Energetic Healer at TheHormoneHarmonizer.com

Permissions

Acknowledgments

This book would never have been created without the contributions of many important people. I am deeply grateful to all of the support I've received in birthing this work! Thank you to:

My clients. I have been moved and humbled to witness the brave work of so many beautiful souls. Each person who comes to me for coaching is both gift and guide to me. Thank you for your faith in me and your trust in the process. It is my honor to be present to your expansion.

My parents, Mary Lou and Rick Schneider, have been the best mom and dad a woman could hope for. Each of you has encouraged me to follow my dreams. Dad, you are a constant source of inspiration and hope to me. Thanks for all you've taught me about integrity in business and life,and for keeping me from taking myself too seriously. I know you're having fun and inspiring many in the Otherworld. Mom, what an amazing blessing to be able to work with you, teach with you and share ideas with you! You have blazed a trail for me in so many ways. Thanks for all your love and support and for doing the final edit on my transcript too!

My mentor and soul sister, Dr. Samantha St. Julian. Sami, as you read this book you will recognize so much of yourself in it. Thank you for opening my eyes to the layered and complex nature of reality. Thanks for being there for me through several processes of disintegration and re-integration. For expanding my intuition and challenging me always to break out of my old boxes. For going with me to places no one else would go. I can't imagine who I would be if I hadn't met you. There aren't words, really. Namaste.

Baeth Davis. Thank you for helping me clarify my life purpose and for challenging me to move past my fears and step out into the world.

My coaching groups for supporting me in my process of expansion: Sam, Pat ("Zeus"), Helen, Pat, Mara, Leslie, Dawna, Natalie, Daria, Geanine, Jennifer, Lindsay, Kirsten, Renee, Cathy, Robyn, Joyce, Chantal, Tai, Heather, Sue, Don, Coco, Cherry, Isabel, Gildart, Melora, Ileana, Barbara and Karen.

My informal editors, Daria Boissonnas, Laura Edwards, Todd Edwards, Mary Lou Schneider and David Willis, for your time, your energy and your insights. You helped make my work better. I am deeply grateful!

My copy editor, Jennifer Bloome. You brought so much brilliance to the book...you truly went above and beyond. Thank you for shining your light on this work!

My book designer and photographer, Liz Schneider of Ravenlight Studios. Thank you for assisting me in making the book appealing to the eye and for helping bring my concepts to life.

My proofreader, Linda Austin. Thank you for your conscientiousness and attention to detail.

Eileen Kinsella, who taught me how to trust my own instincts about how to parent both of my wonderfully atypical children. You saw the magic in Bridget from the first moment. Thank you for helping me trust that I had what I needed to walk with her on this journey. And for always encouraging me to write about it!

Our daughter, Maddie, who is a brilliant and beautiful light in my life. You are an extraordinary young woman, and you inspire me constantly with your creative insights. I want to be more like you.

Our daughter, Bridget, who taught me how to consciously manifest. You awakened me to my life's work. Your joy and determination are infectious. I'm so happy I get to be your mom.

David, my husband, partner and friend. Thank you for believing in me. Thanks for listening to all my ideas, reading excerpts and for taking care of the kids when I was writing. You are a wonderful source of support and the place I always come back to when I want to remind myself how great it is to be alive. I have so much fun with you. Journeying together just keeps getting better. I love you.

A note about confidentiality: I respect the confidentiality of my clients. The stories you will read in here are either composite characters created by common themes I witnessed in many different people, or they are from clients and friends who've given me permission to share their experiences.

About the Author

What do you get when you take a person with the soul of a poet, the mind of a scholar and the heart of a healer-and turn her into a trial lawyer? Existential crisis and more graduate school! Throw in some transformational life experiences and decades of coaching extraordinary individuals to consciously create meaningful lives, and you end up with Kimberly Schneider, The Manifestation Maven. Kimberly has empowered thousands of disenchanted dreamers to create magic and miracles here and now through her Cornucopia Method of Manifestation.

A former trial attorney and psychotherapist, Kimberly has also developed courses and offered ongoing and on-the-spot instruction in ethics, impactful communication, innovative and strategic thinking, psychology, personal growth, creative expression, law, information marketing, entrepreneurship, sales, intentional languaging (mindfully using speech to create successful outcomes) and positive thinking. Kimberly is a professional speaker with over thirty years of in-depth, varied experience ranging from courtrooms, commencement addresses and business meetings to motivational speeches, workshops and seminars, retreats, television appearances, radio interviews, audios, internet videos and tele-seminars. She enjoys engaging with and inspiring audiences.

An Adjunct Lecturer of Communication at Washington University in St. Louis, Kimberly appears regularly as a guest expert on *Great Day St. Louis* television show and hosts the *Conscious Manifesting* show on WebTalkRadio.net. In addition to publishing her own blogs and e-newsletters, she has contributed to numerous publications including *Wealth Magazine's* newsletter and *The Healthy Planet*.

Kimberly's unique blend of original poetry, storytelling and innovative, practical tools for transformation make her a powerful speaker. She enjoys interacting with audience members on the spot and empowering people to break through the illusions that keep them stuck. Her keynote speeches, workshops and retreats evoke laughter, tears and life-altering awareness. Kimberly also offers customized coaching programs for individuals and groups, including one and two day Soul Retrieval programs. You can experience a taste of Kimberly's style on *Terrible Beauty: Poems and Reflections for Precarious Times,* an audiobook of poetry and insights designed to support, heal and empower people during life's challenges (available through Avalon Emerging Press at **KimberlySchneider.com**).

Kimberly's favorite childhood book was an encyclopedia about the Seven Wonders of the Ancient World. She has been devouring ancient historical fiction since middle school and majored in Classical Studies. Thirty hours of Latin and courses like The Legal System in Ancient Greece, Comparative Ancient Religions and The History of Sparta didn't seem to have a lot of practical value, but she sure loved them! As an adult she shifted her attention from stories of Alexander the Great and the Romans to the cultures they conquered. Soon she developed a passion for exploring indigenous spirituality, including the worldview of the Celts. Kimberly facilitates a weeklong workshop on the coast of western Ireland exploring Irish cosmology and Celtic spirituality through poetry, myth, mysticism, music, the elements and primeval places of power. **KimberlySchneider.com/trips**

Kimberly and her husband have two extraordinary children, both of whom have played pivotal roles in her spiritual growth and in the development of The Cornucopia Method of Manifestation. Their family's household motto is "Normal Is Overrated."

*Author photo by Lindsay Miller

How to Contact the Author

Kimberly offers transformational keynote speeches and customized workshops, coaching, training and consulting in life and business alchemy, innovative thinking, intuition and communication. For more information about Kimberly and her programs see **KimberlySchneider.com**

Please direct inquiries to:

Kimberly Schneider
1324 Clarkson/Clayton Center, Ste. 177,
St. Louis, MO 63011
support@KimberlySchneider.com | **KimberlySchneider.com**
314-275-8188

Additionally, Kimberly welcomes letters and emails from readers with questions, comments and suggestions for future books. Please email **support@KimberlySchneider.com** or "like" Kimberly's manifestation page on Facebook and post to her there at **Facebook.com/KimberlyVSchneider** If you'd like to receive Kimberly's free *Conscious Life Creation e-Course*, you can request it at **TheManifestationMaven.com**.

Contents

Foreword

This important and essential manual of lifestyle is well and truly named and one of the rare, skillful books that actually delivers what it promises. All the wisdom for embracing a life fully animate and thriving, open to the spiritual in the widest sense, is beautifully articulated here.

As I browsed through this book initially, the words of two other geniuses of writing came to mind: one, a second century Christian saint, Ireneus; the other, a twenty-first century philosopher and poet, John O'Donohue.

Ireneus made the magnificent pronouncement that "the Glory of God is every single person fully alive;" John, on the other hand, describes that rare transformative moment of new beginning when we emerge out of old ways of thinking because of something we read, hear or sense, and that is what simply happens after reading Kimberly's acute self-awareness here. "You can trust the promise of this opening...awaken your spirit to adventure...for your soul senses the world that awaits you"

Furthermore, Kimberly is a beautiful poet and her inspiring poems woven into her marvelous manual lie naturally and easily beside the words of Jalaluddin Rumi, Meister Eckhart and Mahatma Gandhi, making *Everything You Need Is Right Here* a treasure trove of artistic creativity as well as a cornucopia of right living.

Pick up this book, read it, re-read it – aloud if you can at all – and transform your heavy, overburdened, fearful heart of stone into a noble fleshy heart of great compassion, huge forgiveness and immense, boundless love.

One more vital advice from me-one who is convinced of the crucial significance of this book in our troubled world and who was deeply moved, stimulated and transformed through the reading and contemplating:

Pass this literary jewel on to at least five of your loved ones.

Because once **YOU** have really read and cherished Kimberly's unique insights and understanding of the essence of being fully human and alive, you can now for the first time really **LOVE** yourself which, in turn, frees you to lavish that same love on your neighbour.

In short, this outstanding, exceptional treasure trove is the perfect articulation of the Golden Rule of ALL religions or deep philosphical wisdom: *Love your neighbour as yourself.*

Noirin Ni Riain, Ph.D.
Glenstal Abbey,
Murroe, Co. Limerick, Ireland
Author of *Theosony: Towards a Theology of Listening*
   and *Listen with the Ear of the Heart: A Biography*

How to Use This Book

Everything You Need Is Right Here is a book that has the power to totally transform your life. Now truth be told, that could be said about a lot of books, and perhaps you've experienced that before. However, I'm going to encourage you to approach this book in a different way than you've probably interacted with books in the past.

I used to offer much of the material in this book as a $297 Home Study Course. Why did I charge that much for the Home Study Course, and why have I released it now as a book, at a much lower cost? Those are good questions. They deserve answers.

I've noticed something interesting about how people tend to use books they can buy for under $25, even people highly invested in their personal and spiritual development. They may enjoy the books, be inspired by them, even recommend them to other people...yet not make any real changes based on what they've read. Why is that? First, it may have to do with the way we usually read. Most of what we take in through one sense (seeing or hearing, for instance) is lost after a short time. We usually need to incorporate two or more senses and also repeat information in many different ways in order for it to become anchored in our consciousness deeply enough to produce real changes. And the vast majority of us won't do that with a $25 book. However, *if we actually work with the concepts in a book via exercises, more like a class or a course, then the ideas can take root and flourish.*

That's why I originally created a Home Study Course for this material. I knew the concepts were life changing and I'd also seen that when people invest more of themselves in something, it makes a bigger impact. So I sold the Home Study Course for $297. After a couple of years of watching people make transformational changes in their lives using this information, including The Manifestation Matrix Meditation, I knew I wanted to make it available to a larger

3

audience. And more people shop at bookstores than purchase home study courses. So, now you have it: $297 worth of material for about one tenth of the price. (AND, bonus: I've even added some new stuff).

Please don't let the small investment you've made in this book allow you to treat it as a minor event. Frankly, the concepts in here are worth much more than $297...but only, of course, if you implement them into your day-to-day life! So treat it like a class. Do the exercises, and talk about what you're learning with others.

Intellectual knowledge is worth nothing without practical application. My hope for you is that the experience I'm inviting you to step into – the experience of what I call the Cornucopia Reality- comes alive for you. I can promise you – *absolutely promise you* – that it will happen, if you consistently use the tools I'll be giving you, even when it is difficult. Especially when it is difficult. When you do that, you're in for a nice surprise. You'll discover that the difficulty was of your own making, and that ease and joy were there for you all the time. Waiting for you to stop resisting. So, here are a few tips to help you integrate the concepts and the tools:

1. **Read through the entire book first**. Then, read it again and do the exercises. Some of the ideas are a bit complex. Don't worry – you'll get them, if that is important to you. I will offer lots of examples and explain things in multiple ways. What's more, you don't even need to understand the concepts in order to make them work for you. If you read the book once for familiarity, then come back to the material a second time, you will be better prepared to use all of the tools.

2. Please, **write out the exercises**. Writing will do a few things for you. First, you'll integrate the material even more by writing. Second, the exercises are there so you can begin taking action on changing the way you think, feel and behave. If you take the time to reflect on each

exercise and write out your answers, you'll be giving yourself an opportunity to expand your consciousness and change your life. Third, if you write out your answers to the exercises it will give you some perspective later. You might even want to put dates by each of your answers. It will be fun for you to look back someday and see how much your life has changed since you started working with The Cornucopia Method of Manifestation.

3. As you read through the book, **keep a pen and a highlighter handy** so you can copy important points to your journal (see tip number four, below) and add your own notations for future reference.

4. If you really want to take your learning to the next level, **get a special journal** to chronicle your adventure through consciousness. Make gratitude lists, write down your goals and dreams, jot down notes about your meditation experiences. Journal about your big aha's as well as the material that challenges, triggers and stretches you. Have fun chronicling how your dreams come to fruition in more amazing and wonderful ways than you ever imagined. Finally, be sure to make note of the positive changes you see in yourself and in your life along the way.

5. **Engage in a regular meditation practice**, starting with The Manifestation Matrix Meditation. You will learn more about the meditation later. For now I'll just say this: the more you do it, the easier conscious manifestation will be for you. You have access to a free audio of this meditation at **kimberlyschneider.com/manifestationmatrixaudio**. Download that and you'll have my voice to guide you through the meditation whenever you like. You can download the audio directly to your computer and then put it on an mp3 player or burn it to a CD, whichever is most convenient for you.

6. **If ever you feel stuck** while working through the book, jump ahead for a bit to Part Three, which highlights the four obstacles to conscious manifestation (resistance, judgment, guilt/blame and pretending, in case you were wondering). One of my friends suggested these four obstacles were so important they ought to be at the beginning of the book. I decided to leave them at the end, because it is critical to remember that the obstacles will continue to pop up, even when you are working the five steps of The Cornucopia Method of Manifestation. But due to his suggestion (thanks Todd!) I wanted to at least let you know those obstacles are explained in Part Three.

7. **Form a group** to discuss the book, share your insights and support each other in applying the concepts. Eighty-five percent of what you hear or read one time will be lost within two weeks UNLESS you do something to anchor it in your consciousness. The more ways you can enhance your learning of this material, the faster and easier your process will be. Read the book, listen to The Manifestation Matrix Meditation, write about your experiences and talk about The Cornucopia Method of Manifestation with positive, open-minded people.

Innovation expert Alan Deutschman lists three elements to successful, long-lasting change in his book *Change or Die*:
   o *relating* to someone who inspires and encourages you,
   o *reframing* your experiences in ways that change your thinking and support your growth, and
   o *repeating* new ways of thinking and doing until they become natural.
All three key elements of change are included in this book to ensure that you will be successful.

I've written this book in a conversational style. I also chose to record The Manifestation Matrix Meditation audio myself because I want you to get to know me. So it may not be as polished or perfect as it would be with a professional actor reading it, but I want you to have the living vibration of my voice and my familiarity with the material right there with you. I'll be sharing some personal things about my life and what I learned from them in ways that will give you hope and courage. I will be journeying with you as you move through the book.

I'll give you insights and exercises to help you reframe your thinking. You'll recognize beliefs that once served you but are now holding you back, and you will be able to let them go.

And there's plenty of repetition here. If you complete the whole book and do the suggested exercises, you will know this material. Your body, mind and spirit will absorb the concepts. Your left and right brain will integrate the ideas. Your life will be utterly transformed.

So grab your pen and highlighter right now and dive in. Make a commitment to yourself to do the exercises for whatever you cover in the book within 24 hours of reading each chapter.

Enjoy!

Introduction

Promises of The Cornucopia Method: Results You Can Expect

This book is the result of over forty years of lived experimentation in conscious manifestation. Okay, I admit the first eighteen years or so I was fairly unconscious about all of this stuff, but I've made up for it in the last two-plus decades.

My intention for you is that after reading this book, actively engaging in the exercises, listening to The Manifestation Matrix Meditation audio and applying the principles in your own life (which I'm going to show you exactly how to do) you will experience these results:

You will notice an almost-immediate improvement in your ability to consciously direct the course of your life.

You will be happier, freer and more at peace.

You will experience more of whatever abundance means to you: time, freedom, health, love, wonder, joy, serenity, faith, knowledge or money (or, ideally, all of those things).

You will take delight in your creative power and develop the capacity to marvel at it, even when what you are experiencing is less than pleasant.

Your thoughts will be positive for longer and longer periods of time.

You will have tools at your disposal to help you recognize when you are out of alignment with your deepest desires and to take immediate action to get yourself back on track.

*Magic and miracles will become a regular part
of your existence.*

You will enjoy life more.

As a speaker, counselor and Life and Business
Alchemist/Coach, I've worked with many people who are
frustrated. They come to me because they've watched
movies or read books about manifestation or the Law of
Attraction. They like the ideas, but feel they can't make it
work for them.

It seems easy to talk about manifestation when you like
what you are living. When you are faced with unpleasant or
painful life situations, however, it can be challenging to take
responsibility for creating your life.

When I hear clients say, "This manifestation stuff
doesn't work for me," what they really mean is they don't
like what they are currently manifesting. And I can't blame
them for feeling frustrated and unhappy, since what many
of them seem to believe about manifestation is this:

I'm responsible for creating my reality – and my life sucks.

*Therefore, it must be my fault that these horrible things are
happening to me.*

However, some of those assumptions are wrong. In fact,
I have some good news for you:

Whatever is happening in your life is not a punishment.

This book is not about beating yourself up because
you've been thinking bad thoughts. In fact, if you can let go
of self-judgment you'll begin to see that every moment in
your life holds a doorway to joy. (And don't worry, I'm
going to tell you how to let go of self-judgment.)

When you are ready to take full responsibility for everything that happens in your experience without judgment or blame, when you can truly accept that you are the producer, director and actor in this movie you call your life, then you are fully empowered to make changes.

In fact, incredible as it may seem, everything you need to create ultimate fulfillment is right here, right now, in this moment. *Everything you need is right here.* All you need to do is awaken your consciousness to see it.

Are you ready for the challenge? Are you ready to get clear about who you really are and what you'll have the most fun creating? And are you ready to see it happen?

I thought so!

Let's get started.

A Few Words about Money and God

This book is not about money. It's about manifesting magic and miracles. Having access to plenty of money is just one aspect of abundant manifestation. You may have purchased this book to learn how to have better relationships or vibrant health or to figure out what makes you happy.

However, most of the people who seek my services as a speaker and Life and Business Alchemist/Coach end up coming around to money at some point. It's true that money alone won't make you happy. And yet, abundant finances can free you up to focus on what does make you happy.

Our culture has a strange relationship with money. Most people want more of it, and yet they feel guilty about having that desire. How many times have you heard someone insist that they aren't doing something for the money, but instead for some other (presumably more altruistic) reason?

It feels nice to think that your motives are pure. And there are lots of social benefits to doing good. It's important to realize though, that everything you do, no matter how

11

well-meaning, regardless of whether you earn money for it or not, arises from a basic desire to be happy and to feel good. Whether you're volunteering at the soup kitchen, giving a speech, driving kids to school, making dinner, working with a client or visiting someone in the hospital, there's some sort of personal pay-off. *You* benefit. Even if what you are doing doesn't feel good at all, some part of you receives a payoff from your behavior. Or you wouldn't do it.

On the other hand, even if you are clear that you do want more money, it's important to understand that no one does anything for money alone. The money itself is a non-issue; it's what the money stands for that counts. For some, money is a means to an end. It is a form of exchange that can give you opportunities to surround yourself with beauty, enjoy new experiences, give you access to information and resources and allow you the freedom to spend the time doing things you enjoy. For others, money represents security, love, appreciation or something else.

I've worked with hundreds of entrepreneurs, many of them helping professionals (bodyworkers, therapists, doctors, counselors, instructors) who have struggled with the idea that getting paid well for what they do somehow diminishes the integrity of their work. Some of these people could barely pay their bills when they first came to me. Their experiences of scarcity and anxiety around money impacted how well they were able to perform their important and healing work. And as a healer myself, I have often felt conflicted about how to place a monetary value on what I offer the world.

If you, too, have money issues, (and I've encountered precious few who don't), then this book may push some buttons for you. In fact, I'd be disappointed if it didn't. If your buttons are pushed, it's likely you've touched on a belief that's been getting in the way of your dreams. If you can stay with the process, you'll be able to release the limiting beliefs that have been driving your attitudes and behaviors. You'll be able to break through whatever has been holding you back.

Conscious Manifestation Secret

Whenever you have a strong reaction to anything you read in this book, I invite you to stop and take a deep breath. See if you can move into a state of curiosity. Notice the chatter happening in your mind about what you've read. Take another breath. Where is your body registering the emotional intensity? Place your hand there. Keep breathing. Let your mind chatter on. Say to yourself, *I notice discomfort here.* Keep breathing. Now return to the content that triggered your discomfort and re-evaluate it, or come back to it later. You were drawn to this book—you can do this!

Please understand, I'm not suggesting that you should agree with everything in this book, or even that you need to agree with me in order to benefit from its contents. But I'll be happy for you if you can discern what's true for you from a place of neutrality rather than reactivity.

I know for myself that whenever I'm testing out new ideas there is a period of confusion. (These days, when I recognize this happening, I get excited because it means I'm on the verge of expanding). It's like the first time my Pilates instructor told me to use my belly to move my leg. I had no idea what she was talking about. But she reassured me that uncertainty was normal, that my body just needed to learn a new way of moving. She encouraged me to stay with it, to try on the idea that my belly could move my leg, even if I didn't understand how that could happen. Her support allowed me to hang in there through that baffling period when I simply didn't get it. In fact, for a few moments it seemed like my brain quit working altogether and I forgot how to move at all! Now I can easily move my leg with my belly. But when I started, there were many moments when I questioned why I ever thought Pilates was a good idea.

13

Let this book be for you what my Pilates teacher was for me. Allow the ideas here to be your template for creating meaning in the midst of not knowing. It's easier to let go of old ways of being if you can hold on to a new way (however temporarily) during the process.

You may have heard the expression that "money is energy." I like to say that money is a vehicle for the energetic exchanges you make. Because most of those exchanges are unconscious, money carries your projected thoughts, beliefs, attitudes and emotions.

So, if you work through your money issues, you may find that you've worked through all your issues. It's a worthy task, and you are worth the fortitude it requires. This book should get you well on your way.

Now that we've touched on money, let's deal with another hot button: God. I hesitate to use the word at all since it carries so much charge. So sometimes I refer to the Divine as the All That Is, the Cosmic Consciousness or Christ Consciousness (oops — that "C" word can be problematic too).

But I will be talking about it. Money and God are intimately related.

Here's the thing. I have no need to change your beliefs about whatever you call that Energy that runs through everything. It can continue to live for you as BuddhaMind, God, Christ, Allah, Goddess, Brahman, Universe, the Higher Conscious Mind, the Superconscious, Source Energy (you get the idea). And it's fine even if you don't believe there is such a thing as a Supreme Consciousness at all.

Just understand that I'm going to use whatever words appeal to me at the time I'm writing a particular section. Some of these ideas may seem heretical to you. I am not writing to convert anyone, but to share what has worked for me and for my clients.

My thoughts about manifesting are loosely tied together by the paradigm I'm living in at the moment. This paradigm makes sense to me now and gives my mind a useful vehicle for navigating through life. I have lived long enough to expect it to change. Take what you like, substitute words or concepts as necessary and *consciously* create a way of viewing reality that makes sense to you out of the ideas that resonate. Leave the rest.

Questioning your old, unexamined assumptions about who you are and what you are capable of creating will stir up some inner conflict. Rejoice in it. In all likelihood, the discomfort is arising from the part of you that has kept you small. (That part is often afraid of expansion).

You don't have to believe any of this. I invite you to try my methods and watch what happens. If they don't work for you, then your process may reinforce your current beliefs. If, however, your process pushes you to expand, if you enter a new and exiting reality, well, then...a little discomfort is a small price to pay to be admitted to the Valley of Your Wildest Dreams.

What Is The Cornucopia Method of Manifestation?

The cornucopia is one of the oldest symbols of abundance.

You'll see it at Thanksgiving time in the U.S.: a cone-shaped basket filled with squash, pumpkins, pomegranates, corn and other fruits of autumn.

The Thanksgiving cornucopia, however, with its suggestion of plentiful food to sustain us through the winter, only hints at the ancient power that the symbol represents.

The word "cornucopia" comes from Latin terms meaning "horn of plenty." According to Greek mythology, the first horns of plenty rested on the head of Amaltheia, a fairy goat who nursed the infant god Zeus. The horns produced nectar and ambrosia and helped Zeus grow into the most powerful deity on Mount Olympus. When Amaltheia died, Zeus gave her horns to the nymphs who helped raise him. The magical horns retained their powers—they could never be emptied. Amaltheia's horn, the cornucopia, became a symbol of inexhaustible bounty, freely bestowed by the gods.

I've always loved ancient history and mythology. I studied Classics in college and I've scoured ancient stories all my life for esoteric truths. So when I began learning about how manifestation works, the story of Amaltheia's horn of plenty came to mind. The more I worked with the idea of an unlimited Source, the more I realized that this truth was at the heart of all the teachings on manifestation. And perhaps this teaching is exactly what we need to set our species free.

After all, if every one of us truly does have access to the Source of all Creation, and if that Source is unlimited, then there is nothing to fear. There is no need to struggle, attack or defend.

We need not dispute territories or worry about whether there is enough food, water or energy. Our species has the capacity to create whatever we need. We can wake up to a world with plenty of healthy food and clean water, meaningful work for all who want it and thriving, dynamic ecosystems all over the planet. We can live in peace, reveling in our diversity while also creating meaningful connections. We can transform our fear into courage and our doubt into trust. We can walk in beauty.

If only we could remember how to do it.

Ah, how to do it. That's the trick, yes? That's what this book will teach you.

Of course, I am by no means the first person to recognize the essential truth symbolized by the cornucopia.

In the last 100 years teachers like Wallace Wattles, Florence Scovel Shinn, Catherine Ponder, Napoleon Hill and many others have taught that all human beings have direct access to infinite resources (Source energy) and that we create our reality with our thoughts and are therefore capable of changing our reality as we change our thoughts. More recently, Louise Hay, Deepak Chopra, Esther and

Jerry Hicks, Sonia Choquette, Gregg Braden, Alan Cohen and other authors have resurrected what I call the "cornucopia concepts," teaching people how to consciously manifest.

Most people who teach about manifestation talk about the Law of Attraction. Essentially, the Law of Attraction means that like attracts like. Everything in our universe is energy and everything vibrates at a very particular energetic frequency. Therefore, everything that happens in your life — let me say that again — *everything that happens in your life* occurs because you are emitting certain energetic frequencies, and those frequencies attract experiences that are energetically resonant. Since time usually passes between your dispersion of a particular frequency and the arrival of its energetic answer, it can be difficult to determine how a particular event was set into motion by your thoughts, emotions and feelings.

If these ideas seem far out to you, consider that 2,000 years ago Jesus was teaching that all you need do to have whatever you wish for is to ask. "After all, if you asked your Father for bread, would He give you a stone?" (Matthew 7:9; Luke 11:11).

At this point you are probably thinking, *That sounds great in theory, but take one look at my life and you'll see that my wishes have definitely NOT all been granted!* And you might be right, if only the clearest wishes of your conscious mind went into the mix. But with your unconscious mind acting as a mediator between your conscious mind and the Creative Source, most of what occurs in your life is a result of what lives in your unconscious. And, as a former psychotherapist, I would argue that if you put your conscious wishes under close scrutiny you would find that even there you have many conflicting desires.

You, and most of humanity, have been trapped in a reality that has not allowed you to believe in your own creative power. While you were born with direct access to every good thing, most of the time you are manifesting the best that your unconscious mind can hope for within its beliefs of scarcity.

When you can't conceive of a universe where you are the author of your reality, you hide from your own power. You project it onto (and hand it over to) events and situations outside of yourself, calling them fate, luck, other people or God.

And this is why many people who are learning about the Law of Attraction are unable to master it, because they can't seem to break through the deeply held beliefs that cage them in a passive life experience. In order to step into your power completely, you must transcend that reality once and for all. You must transform those limiting beliefs into attitudes that enable you to experience your connection to the cornucopia.

My Story

I've always had a knack for manifesting, although when I was younger I would not have used that language.

In most areas of my life, I could decide I wanted to achieve a particular goal or have something happen and then set out to realize my dream. Usually, it worked. I was not conscious of exactly what I was doing to make this happen, or that there was anything unusual about it.

In my early thirties, I had a telephone reading with a psychic named Jim who told me, "Wow. Your energy is unique. You are one of the most powerful, effective manifesters I have ever worked with."

Honestly, I didn't know what he was talking about. Manifester? I had to ask him to define the word.

"You can take ideas and make them happen, right?" asked Jim. "You imagine something and then you create it."

Well, yes. I did do that. Didn't everyone?

According to Jim, apparently not.

I was fascinated. What, exactly, was I doing? And if I could figure that out, wouldn't I be able to make my life even better?

That's when my exploration of conscious manifestation began, but it would be some time later before everything I was learning would be put to the test.

Winter Solstice, 2001. Our youngest daughter, Bridget, had a cough. For most kids this would not be worrisome, but Bridget had a congenital heart defect, developmental delays and a diagnosis of failure to thrive. She sounded like she was drowning in phlegm. I knew that her compromised heart function and oxygen capacity could be impairing her ability to throw off whatever illness she was harboring. So I took her to the pediatrician.

By this time in Bridget's eighteen months of life, I was adept at going to the doctor. She had been through every diagnostic test you can think of: cranial CT, MRI, EEG, multiple blood draws. She'd had open-heart surgery and cardiac catheterization. She'd seen a myriad of specialists and I knew more about pediatric medicine than I had ever wanted to learn.

Bridget's nurse, Barb, took a pulse oxymeter reading. I saw the numbers and I knew the oxygen levels were too low. Barb confirmed that the levels justified hospitalization. She said she'd come back with the doctor in about fifteen minutes and if the levels had not gone up, we'd be off to Children's Hospital.

Four days until Christmas. I had another child at home who was looking forward to Santa and presents, family and fun. And I was now facing the prospect of a holiday in the hospital.

I opened a magazine and began reading to distract myself and pass the time.

I'm still not sure what came over me, but as I sat there reading and not really taking anything in, something broke through my mind-chatter and said, "Pay attention to what's happening here. Stay with it." So I did. I closed the magazine and sat with what I was feeling and thinking. I looked at my fears about Bridget's immediate health and her long-term prognosis. I thought about all I had to get done for the holidays. I watched the chatter get quieter and quieter. And then I saw what was underneath all of that.

And I have to tell you, I was horrified.

When I was honest with myself I could see that part of me was addicted to the drama of all this. As bizarre as it sounds, some small part of me was looking for her to be sick. I had been defining myself in relationship to Bridget's problems: The mother who could handle whatever happened with grace and aplomb. The woman who could talk to the doctors in their own language and prompt the question, "Are you in the medical field?" The mother who would do anything to help her daughter overcome.

I didn't want it to define me anymore, this piece of myself that I saw. Frankly I didn't want to associate with it at all, but there it was.

Somehow in those few minutes between my epiphany and when the nurse came back, I was able to find some compassion for myself. I saw that my ego had found an effective way to cope with all I had dealt with since Bridget's birth. I had become an expert at crisis and drama and I did it really well. So I forgave myself for my humanness and then I got really clear that what I wanted most for Christmas was for my daughter to be home and healthy. A few moments later, the nurse came back in and took Bridget's oxygen levels again. They had gone up dramatically. We went home and Bridget's cough cleared up in time for Christmas.

Did I make Bridget's oxygen levels go up? Bridget certainly influences her own reality, so I'm not prepared to say I was wholly responsible for the change. But I'm not prepared to say I didn't influence the outcome either. What I do know is that times of emotional intensity contain enormous power to move us forward toward what we truly desire, if we approach them with understanding.

As you can imagine, Bridget's life and our family's search for healing has produced some great stories. You'll read more about her in this book. Her journey thus far would be a great stand-alone book (perhaps I'll do that one another time...). But I refer to her now because living with Bridget has been instrumental in my development of The Cornucopia Method of Manifestation. Mothering Bridget has been my university for deepening my understanding of conscious manifestation, experiencing the sometimes miraculous benefits, and wanting to share it with others. As of 2011, Bridget is eleven years old and she's thriving. She's had five open heart surgeries and her heart is stable. She is happy and healthy. Her development is progressing nicely.

In this period of relative calm I've had the luxury to review my experiences and consider what I've learned about manifestation. I've studied the masters, scouring and devouring every resource I could get my hands on about manifestation and the Law of Attraction and pondered how those concepts were operating when Bridget's life seemed to hang in the balance. I've looked very carefully at what worked and what didn't. This powerful combination of knowledge and trial by fire produced the manifestation method I now teach: The Cornucopia Method of Manifestation.

You're now reading the first book designed to teach this proven method.

My ability to manifest consciously has increased exponentially since I began utilizing this method, and my clients have had similar results.

I haven't yet managed to move objects with my mind or produce ash in my hand like Sai Baba, but I'll keep you posted. Our species is on the verge of explosive evolution. Dr. David Hawkins, who has developed a method of measuring human awareness, reports in his book, *Power vs. Force,* that our collective consciousness has expanded suddenly and exponentially in the last thirty years. And it makes sense, doesn't it? It had to happen eventually. After all, according to many accounts, Jesus cured the blind, healed the sick, walked on water and raised the dead. And he said that we'd do even greater things (John 14:12).

That means you, too.

Are you ready to raise the dead? Or do something even greater?

I am excited for you right now as you embark on your own journey of possibility with these concepts. I've written this book with the intention that you'll feel me right there beside you. I'd like you to imagine that when you read my words, I'm speaking directly to you, because I am. I'm telling you the same things I'd say if you were on the other end of the phone line or looking into my eyes at one of my events. I have woven my prayers and highest intentions for you into the crafting of this book. May it support you in making magic and miracles.

Abundant Blessings,

Kimberly Schneider
TheManifestationMaven.com

Part One

The Mechanics of Manifestation

What Is Manifestation?

Manifestation is the process of turning ideas into form. Let's start by taking a look at what we consider "form."

Our known universe is made up of energy. We can perceive or observe energy in two ways: waves (fields of potential) and particles (bits of matter). What's really fascinating is that all matter has both wave (possibility) and particulate (manifested) qualities. In other words, matter holds the possibility of being what it is, and being something else, at the same time.

Moreover, waves and particles exist in multiple realities and levels of form, each resonating at a different frequency of vibration. This is really good news. It means you can approach manifestation in many different ways. You have a variety of entry points available for accessing your reality and for changing it. At first, you may find some levels of reality easier to get into than others, so choose your favorite level as a starting point. Many of these multiple levels of form and vibration also resonate with each other, so by bringing your awareness to one level, you can start a cascade effect. And if you have NO IDEA what I'm talking about right now, please don't worry. I'm going to give you simple tools that will allow you to do this, even if you don't understand HOW you are doing it. More about that later…

Every object and being, from the most solid to the most ephemeral, projects a certain energetic frequency or rate of vibration. In material objects this frequency can be measured in a variety of ways, but even non-material forms like thoughts and emotions have a particular vibration. The vibrational frequency of emotion and thought is what you notice when you sense the energy of a place or a group of people.

Have you ever walked into a room and had the experience of dense energy? Or uplifting energy? Perhaps you've said, *I could have cut the tension with a knife,* or *That place had good vibes.* The vibrational frequency of emotion and thought is what you notice when you sense the energy of a place or group. While an individual thought or emotion may be difficult to detect consciously, the collective thoughts and emotions of a group create more tangible energy that is more easily perceived.

How about the physical world around us? What you experience as the real world of form is a result of collective thought patterns that have become less "wave" and more "particle," so that they are dense enough to be perceived.

Consider a big architectural structure, say the St. Louis Arch. At some point, the Arch was just an idea. Someone wanted to recognize St. Louis as the Gateway to the West via the travels of explorers Lewis and Clark. So committees were formed and the energy grew. In typical bureaucratic fashion, the idea was tossed around for decades and the energy became somewhat diffuse, but finally an architect was hired. The architect brought new focus and energy to the idea of the monument. He pondered what shape might express the feeling of Americans moving into the great unknown. His energy became focused on the shape of an arch. He added more energy to the thought: designing, sketching, creating a model. The idea then pulled in the energies of the government officials who approved the design. And now the idea gained momentum as it drew on engineering, administrative, communication, manufacturing, transportation and construction energies. Human energy coalesced around the idea of the Arch in the form of gasoline, railroads, typewriters, computers, mathematical calculations, blueprints, hardhats, cranes and steel. Bit by bit, that Arch manifested from a mere thought to a solid physical structure that defines the city of St. Louis.

This same sort of process happens for any solid object you can see, feel, taste or touch. Wave, or possibility energy, becomes denser and denser as actions follow thoughts to bring ideas into form.

However, the reality you engage with your physical senses is not actually as solid as it appears. At a molecular and sub-molecular level, all matter is moving back and forth between wave and particle states at a rate too rapid to be perceived by our senses. According to the latest technologies available to measure microscopic phenomena, the tiniest particles actually blink in and out of existence about seven times each second. The human body, for instance, is made of mostly water and minerals constantly pulsing in and out of form. The space between those pulses is the wave state.

The idea that you are materializing and re-materializing over 400 times per minute may be a little disconcerting, to say the least.

But it also holds the potential for your freedom. Because when you know about the space between the pulses (which, incidentally, you might also experience as the space between your thoughts), then you can enter into the Field of Possibilities. You can consciously connect with the Source of Creation and influence the form around you. When you feed that connection on a regular basis, you are freed from the perception that life happens to you rather than because of you. And with this freedom comes the power to create whatever sort of life you desire.

Why Manifestation?

Imagine that your consciousness is part of a greater, infinite consciousness. This consciousness has been referred to in countless ways, including: Brahman, The Godhead, The Absolute. For now, let's call it Essence. Essence is all there is. It is the force behind creation and it runs through everything in creation. It is the space between things and the things themselves. It is your uniqueness and your connectedness all at once. It is yin and yang swirling together in unity.

Now I will tell you a story as ancient as the universe itself. Come with me to the Time before Time, where Essence experiences a desire to know itself as itself. However, there is no such thing as non-Essence, no contrast against which Essence can understand its being-ness. So

Essence creates an illusion of non-Essence, the illusion of separation, in order to have a field of vision in which to observe itself. But of course, since Essence created the illusion, everything within the illusion is actually made up of (you guessed it) Essence. Flowing from Essence, the illusion continues to grow and evolve. The illusion is beautiful and perfect, even when it appears to be grotesque and flawed, because it is still fully and truly Essence.

What does this have to do with the human experience? We are expressions of Essence. Yet we've become so immersed in the experience of the great Cosmic experiment we're just waking up to the idea that we were part of designing the study!

But why would we have designed it this way? Why would we create a reality in which we'd get lost? Because in order for the experience to be any fun, the various forms that Essence assumes within the illusion of non-Essence must take themselves literally. They must experience only their separation and forget, at least for a while, that they are pieces of Essence. Otherwise, the illusion disintegrates and Essence is back to just being Essence. The appearance of separation is a necessary part of the material experience.

Here's an example. Pretend for a moment you're in a theatre watching the fourth Harry Potter movie, *The Goblet of Fire*. In case you've never read the series or seen the films, the villain, Lord Voldemort, tried to murder Harry as an infant, but the spell backfired and ripped Voldemort's soul from his body. Since that time, Voldemort's personality, preserved as a separate consciousness via the darkest sort of magic, has been searching for a way to return to human form.

In the fourth movie of the series, thirteen years after Voldemort's attack on Harry, the "Dark Lord" has discovered how to regain a body. He must create a potion containing the blood of his enemy, Harry.

You grip the seat in the movie theatre as you watch Voldemort's follower, Wormtail, tie Harry to a tombstone.

Wormtail pulls back Harry's sleeve and brings a knife up to Harry's bare and immobilized arm. As the sharp silver blade slices into flesh, Harry screams.

Your eyes are glued to the macabre scene. Wormtail uses a small vial to capture the blood flowing freely from Harry's wound. A nearby cauldron awaits this last ingredient in a steaming, swirling potion that will resurrect Voldemort's human form. The vial is emptied. Drop by drop, Harry's blood completes the spell.

The potion comes to life and Voldemort slowly emerges from the cauldron in his new body. He breathes deeply through the reptilian nasal slits in his chalky white face. He runs his hands over his newly formed lanky arms and allows his fingers to linger on the smooth head that resembles alabaster more than flesh. He opens his bright red eyes and says:

"Cut! Hey, Daniel, let's do another take, eh? I lost concentration. I'm hungry anyway — how about a break and we'll come back fresh?"

Sort of destroys the experience, doesn't it? We're supposed to forget that we're looking at Daniel Radcliffe and Ralph Fiennes. This is supposed to be Harry and Voldemort! If the movie didn't have the power to pull us in, to make us believe, just for a while, that it was real, why would we want to watch it?

Similarly, if all the aspects of Essence acted like Essence all the time, what would be the point of form? There would be nothing to observe or learn or experience.

"All things, from Brahma the creator down to a single blade of grass – are...simply appearances and not real." Shankara, 9th Century Hindu Philosopher

"What is seen is not the truth..." Kabir, 15th Century Muslim/Hindu Mystic

"One day it will have to be officially admitted that what we christened reality is an even greater illusion than the world of dreams." Salvador Dali

Mystics through the ages have offered various ways of conceptualizing the relationship of Essence to the world of form. Hinduism tells us that matter is "Maya," which means "Illusion." Christianity explains that while we are having a human experience, we perceive Essence as though "through a glass, darkly," but when we leave our bodies we meet Essence "face to face." Regardless of the tradition, the message is always the same: remove the veil and you will see that matter is an illusion.

Seers, shamans and wise ones of old were regarded with respect, and sometimes fear, because they could see through the illusion. Sometimes they could even manipulate it and shift the pulsing web of energy to bring about changes in the world of form: bringing the rain, calling the deer, healing the sick. Magic.

But maybe there's a scientific basis for magic. Maybe magic isn't just for shamans anymore.

We are living through an unprecedented time in recorded human history. The mysteries of the ancient traditions are now available, not only to a few initiates, but to everyone. And increasingly, so is the science that supports and confirms these mysteries. More and more people are ready to see beyond the veil. More people are expressing a desire to consciously shift the strands of Essence that permeate the world of form. More people are ready to begin changing their experiential reality.

Of course, if you believe the mystics, humans have always created their reality. Most of us just never realized we were doing it. And if you aren't yet ready to claim responsibility for creating your own reality (that is, if you'd rather ascribe the events of your life to chance, luck, the will of God or some other outside force), you will still be creating your reality anyway. You'll just be doing it unconsciously, and giving something outside of yourself the credit or blame for the life you are making.

In his book, *The Spontaneous Fulfillment of Desire,* Deepak Chopra explains that Vedic philosophy, an ancient worldview from India that pre-dates Hinduism, offers three levels of reality:

1. **The reality that is filled with physical objects** — this is what people are typically referring to when they talk about what's real, that which you experience with your physical senses.

2. **The reality that is filled with subtle objects** — this is the realm of dreams and most spiritual and intuitive experiences. Sometimes called the astral plane, this is the unseen world or "otherworld" where shamans, seers and saints can travel with ease.

3. **The reality that is filled with nothing but consciousness** – this is the level of Essence — the void that is pregnant with all possibilities.

On the third level, consciousness exists. On the second level, consciousness is aware of itself (the witness). On the first level, consciousness creates. As expressions of consciousness or Essence, human beings operate in all three of these planes, but most of the time we perceive only the first level.

The power of conscious manifestation occurs when you become aware that your consciousness, your existence, is participating in creating your reality.

The Manifestation Matrix

While Essence permeates all matter, as a human being you are capable of perceiving Essence within yourself and all beings. You contain all the elements of manifested reality: you are the originator of experience (Essence), the witness to experience and experience itself, all at the same time.

It's likely that for most of your life your attention has been only on yourself as the experience. You may not have been aware of any other level of reality than the one you were experiencing. You have understood your experience as a personality and perhaps a soul within a body having human life. If you recognized Essence (or God, Brahman, The Absolute) as the originator of experience, you may have seen it as something outside yourself. However, if you have begun to develop the witness aspect of yourself (which you might also call the Essential Self), then perhaps you have begun to see that while the Originator may seem to be outside of you, it is also within.

A matrix (Latin for "womb") is a thing within which something else develops. Human beings, with our (presumably) unique ability of recognizing the consciousness in matter, are manifestation matrices. We create material reality via the interaction between our consciousness and our participation in the world of form. We are agents of manifestation. And anything is possible in The Manifestation Matrix.

When our daughter Bridget was small I couldn't bear to buy her clothes for the next season in case she wasn't alive to wear them. Bridget had a congenital heart defect, and for the first few years her hold on life seemed fragile. But an encounter I had one spring day when she was four years old gave me the courage to start imagining possibilities instead of living in fear of "the inevitable."

I was walking Bridget around our neighborhood in her stroller that morning (she did not begin to walk until the age of five). As I put one foot in front of the other, tears were streaming down my face because we were facing a bleak prognosis. Bridget had already undergone three open heart surgeries. Her case was far from textbook, and the doctors were at a loss to explain why she was experiencing a recurrent, apparently intractible and dangerous condition called subaortic stenosis. Multiple surgeries had not corrected the problem. Options were few.

I'd been listening to Deepak Chopra's audio book, *The Spontaneous Fulfillment of Desire*. One interesting idea he mentioned in the audio was the fact that our cells are dying and new cells are born each moment, so that every seven years or so we have completely new bodies. Because of this, Chopra posited, anything was possible, even at the physical level.

I couldn't help wondering whether, somehow, we could call upon Bridget's healthy heart cells to teach her poorly-functioning cells how to support her physical being more efficiently. I pondered this idea, walking, crying and whispering to myself, step after step, "Anything is possible. Anything is possible. Anything is possible."

As I turned the corner I spotted one of our neighbors working in her yard. I knew Edna by name and saw her often as I walked, but I had never stopped to speak with her. For some reason, on that day she waved me over.

"How is she doing?"

Edna gestured at Bridget and smiled at her. Apparently she'd heard about Bridget from others in the neighborhood. "Well," I said, "She's doing all right. The doctors are giving us some challenging information and we're considering what to do with it."

"Oh," Edna said, "Don't listen to the doctors. Did I ever tell you I had a sister who was born with a lot of problems? The doctors said she wouldn't live more than a few weeks. She's in her sixties now. Anything is possible."

I honestly can't remember how I responded to Edna or whether I managed to say anything at all. I may have been too dumbfounded to speak. Did she really just say back to me the words I had been consoling myself with a couple of minutes before?

That encounter changed my life. It was a powerful and almost immediate demonstration of the Universe responding to my thoughts. It enabled me to move forward no longer believing, but *knowing*, that anything is possible.

Since then, I've experienced those types of encounters with increasing frequency, as I have begun to harness the power of conscious manifestation.

And so can you.

You are an agent of manifestation.

Conscious manifestation happens when you understand how to utilize The Manifestation Matrix. You become aware of the Essence underlying the field of form and you choose to direct it. The greater your awareness of how energy or Essence moves through you and through manifested reality, the greater your capacity for conscious creation. Having read this far, you've already taken one step. The rest of the book will give you even more tools.

Next we're going to look at the different levels of The Manifestation Matrix. Before we begin, though, I want to remind you not to worry if some of the concepts that follow are a bit challenging, at least in the beginning. Unless you happen to be an advanced energy worker, a mystic, a quantum physicist or Vedic philosopher, at least a few of these ideas will be new. That's okay. The first read-through will awaken your understanding. As you move through the book you will integrate the concepts more deeply. And by the time you read the book again and work through the exercises, you will be well on your way to conscious manifestation.

The Chakras
Energy Centers in the Manifestation Matrix

You may be familiar with the seven main chakras of the human body. The chakras are areas of the body where energy is focused. Each energy center is related to particular emotional, physical, spiritual and intellectual qualities in the human system. This ancient understanding of the body's energy has been popularized in the West by Barbara Brennan, Donna Eden, Carolyn Myss and other leaders in the field of vibrational and energetic healing. Whether you perceive the chakras as literal, energetic vortices in the body or metaphors for levels of consciousness, working with them can offer you powerful support in the quest for mindful manifestation.

The Cornucopia Method of Manifestation draws upon the chakra system to improve awareness of how Essence expresses itself in the human form and your role in directing the manifestations of your life. I will offer an overview of the seven basic chakras and what they represent. It is important to remember, however, that while we associate these states of reality with different areas of the human body, in truth they are accessible from any point in the body. The body is filled with consciousness. It is consciousness, and every state of reality contains the seeds of the others.

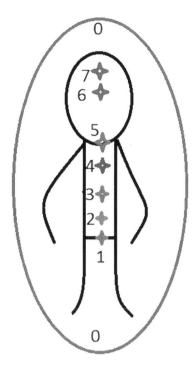

Approximate location of major chakras

Level 0: The Unified Field. Cornucopia Reality. Although Essence permeates all reality and is therefore in every one of the body's energy centers, for ease of discussion and conceptual understanding we will consider Cornucopia Reality separately from the seven individual energy centers. The Unified Field is Level 0, Essence, the reality of pure consciousness. Everything in our universe is made up of the stuff of this reality, which is non-stuff. The Cornucopia Reality exists within, but also beyond all of our manifested experiences. It is the realm of Pure Consciousness within which the illusion of separation is stripped away. This is the Cornucopia. In the Unified Field, we are the candle flames merging into the fiery sun, or the drop of water released into the ocean.

You may notice that I've also assigned the number zero to the Ground Consciousness level, which we will discuss in a few paragraphs. Zero is the number of both beginning and completion. It is the Void and the fullness of creation at the same time. In the Tarot system, the number zero represents the fool, who contains both the innocence of youth and the wisdom of age.

Energy Center 7: The Throne of Consciousness. Essential Reality. The seventh energy center resides in the crown of the head. Mystics have often perceived Essence as entering the body at this energy center. Meditation or mindtraining awakens this chakra, and it is from this point that you come to experience yourself as part of the Cornucopia.

Energy Center 6: Expanded Consciousness. Imaginal Reality. Commonly called the third eye or the brow chakra, this energy center can be perceived just above and between the eyes. The sixth energy center is the part of you that sees beyond what can be detected by the physical senses.

Energy Center 5: Truth Consciousness. Vibrational Reality. The fifth energy center is located in the throat area. It is a Vibrational Reality in that it is associated with sound. Sound holds matter together (thus the origin of the word "universe," which means "one song"). Vibrational Reality enables you to express your unique Truth in the world and begins the process of bringing ideas into form.

Energy Center 4: Emotional Consciousness. Connective Reality. The fourth energy center is located in the heart/thoracic area of the body. It is the middle chakra, the part of The Manifestation Matrix where heaven and earth intersect. It is associated with compassion, healing and the understanding that you are one with everyone and everything. You are connected.

Energy Center 3: Ego Consciousness. Individual Reality. The third energy center is located in the solar plexus/abdominal region. This chakra is associated with will and personal power. It holds both the potential for enslavement to the ego or personality, as well as the ability to harness personal power to serve the greater good.

Energy Center 2: Tribal Consciousness. Relational Reality. The second energy center is located in the pelvis. It holds the imprint of your ancestry and collective consciousness. Here you can experience your instincts to bond with a group, to serve the tribe through procreation and also protect your personal collective from the "other," those who do not look, think or see the world like you do. The energy here also contains the ability to bring creative ideas from the Imaginal Reality (the sixth energy center) into form.

Energy Center 1: Survival Consciousness. Limbic Reality. The first energy center is located in the perineal area, from the tip of the tailbone forward to the genitals. Also called the root chakra, this energy center is intimately concerned with survival of form. Survival Consciousness is triggered when you feel threatened and it can project (typically unconscious) messages of fear and doom into Ground Consciousness (Earth Reality), as explained below.

Level 0: Ground Consciousness. Earth Reality. Essence permeates every level of consciousness, but at this level of reality it gives rise to what you experience as form. Most of the energy directed into the Earth Reality is unconscious. However, the human mind can consciously direct Essence to this level of reality to transmute energy. This is the energetic compost pile—Ground Consciousness has an ability to transform the densest, most troublesome energy into fecund soil that can give rise to bounty.

As previously discussed, the number zero is associated with this level as well as the Unified Field (Cornucopia Reality). I assigned the number zero to both the Cornucopia and Earth Realities to emphasize that every molecule of our material reality is made up of Pure Consciousness: a universe in every cell. Ground Consciousness is a mirror for the Unified Field. It is the Unified Field. It is a reflection of Essence. Our species' historical failure to understand this has resulted in many of our religious traditions dismissing material reality as less important than the world of possibility, or spirit. Now as we recognize the Essential Reality dancing in every particle of creation, as we awaken from the illusion of separation, we are healing the planet and ourselves.

The Cornucopia Method of Manifestation: Let the Universe Work for You

The process of manifestation is not a linear movement from heaven to earth, but a circular communication process between different levels of reality. It is a circuit of energy that is always active, but until you infuse every part of the cycle with consciousness, it is happening (at least in part) without your awareness or consent.

No part of the circuit is more important than any other. Without Matter, Essence loses the ability to experience itself. Without Essence, Matter ceases to be.

Because most people in North America and Western Europe do not use their bodies consciously, they are not grounded. Their awareness resides mostly in the brain, in the mind. They don't fully inhabit their bodies. In my experience, this is one of the biggest contributors to the widespread phenomenon of spiritually-oriented people who seem unable to succeed on a material level. Their upper chakras — those associated with connecting to the Divine, their Essential Selves, their personal truths and the hearts of all beings — are open and active. However, the lower chakras — those that connect people to their personal will, the collective culture and the material world — are blocked or dormant.

Conversely, some people are lower-chakra dominant. When the lower chakras have not been awakened with the awareness of the higher realities, they remain stuck in consciousness of survival, self-centered sexual energy, ego dominance and power over others.

Lest you believe, however, that the energies of the lower chakras are somehow unimportant or inherently destructive, note what happens when conscious mind directs Essence through these same vibrations. We can transmute the energies typically committed to sustenance/survival (first chakra), sexuality (second chakra) and pursuing our ego's agenda (third chakra) for a higher purpose. This is why many religious orders require, at least at certain times, strict obedience to a leader or teacher, along with fasting from sex and particular foods. It is not because sex, eating or following our own will are inherently bad. It is because learning how to discipline and transmute the energy of the lower chakras can create powerful change. For instance, Gandhi redirected these energies to achieve the non-violent release of India from British rule. Without the conscious engagement of the lower chakras, our highest ideals and dreams cannot take material form.

The Cornucopia Method of Manifestation draws upon an understanding of The Manifestation Matrix to infuse every energy center in the body with Essence and to create a conduit between the Unified Field and the Earth Reality. It allows you to set vibrational goals, to recognize energetic vibrations that are out of alignment with your desires and to correct those vibrations. Over time, you will gain more clarity about how your thoughts and vibrations are creating your reality, and you will have more power to change those vibrations quickly and easily. Soon you'll be doing it! But first, I think it's important for you to know how the foundation of the method – The Manifestation Matrix Meditation-–came into being.

The Birth of The
Manifestation Matrix Meditation

Back when I was working one-on-one in my private counseling practice, clients would often ask me how to get what they wanted. "It's simple," I replied. "Just step into the space between your thoughts, bring your intention into that space, then release your attachment to the outcome."

I'm embarrassed to admit that at first I couldn't comprehend why this was so hard for people to understand. Apparently, stepping into the space between thoughts was not something that most people knew how to do. Not to mention releasing attachment to the outcome. And I realized that I didn't know what to tell them. I knew how to do it, but what did I know? What exactly was I doing? And how could I describe it in a way that other people could duplicate?

I spent several years pondering this and working on teachable methods for manifesting and releasing attachment. And I realized several things:

The space between thoughts — The Great Space — is the key. We talked about that space between thoughts in the "What Is Manifestation?" section of the book. It is the state of being we naturally experience several times each second as our physical beings rest between particle pulses and exist as wave states. It is the same place I go in my consciousness when I take journeys to the Otherworld during shamanistic soul retrievals, or do energy work with clients or experience healing myself. It is the listening state experienced during contemplative prayer. It is the mystical moment, the liminal place between the worlds described by the ancient Celts. It is a space beyond space, in a time beyond time. Let's call it The Great Space.

You can train yourself to step into The Great Space. For instance, Buddhist monks and nuns and famous meditation teachers like Deepak Chopra and Thich Nhat Hanh know how to access The Great Space because they have spent decades studying the practice of deep meditation. Nuns and monks in contemplative Christian orders access The Great Space via contemplative prayer. And I can step into The Great Space because I've spent years studying energetic healing, meditation, shamanistic/earth-centered spiritual practices, mysticism and various other psycho-spiritual paths. You can do it too. It just takes practice – and I'm going to show you how in this book. The ability to release attachment to the outcome is a natural side effect from spending time in The Great Space. And proficiency with this ability is a critical step for conscious manifestation.

Stepping into The Great Space while also holding a desired intention and releasing attachment to outcome is a paradoxical experience. It engages several states of being at once. To be specific, this process engages every one of the chakras we explored in the previous section.

To consciously manifest, you must step into The Great Space, which means you are connecting with Pure Consciousness. But if you surrender entirely to your Essential Nature, then any desires you have on a material level will dissolve. So somehow you have to connect with Pure Consciousness without losing yourself in it. You need to maintain enough of your individuality to focus on your manifestation goal. But at the same time, if you allow yourself to let that focus intensify so that it becomes an attachment to outcome, you cut yourself off from Pure Consciousness and that Cornucopia power. Attachment to outcome is evidence of the ego's desire to maintain its happy illusion of control over form.

So conscious manifestation requires:

a) **connection to Unity without surrendering individuality**

41

as well as

b) the ability to maintain a clear vision of your desires as a unique individual without getting lost in your ego's ideas about how those desires will take physical form.

It's quite a trick, really.

Still, I was convinced there must be some straightforward, accessible way to explain this process. I didn't believe that people necessarily needed to spend years in intense meditation training to learn it. I also felt that humanity was ready to step into consciousness of its creative power.

So I began reflecting on my own process of conscious manifestation and how I could duplicate it for others. What was I doing when I manifested so clearly and consciously out of my connection with Essence? What steps had I been taking when that worked really well? And what could I do to make that process even more reliable — and accessible to anyone who wanted to replicate it?

I spent many years contemplating, studying, discussing and observing. After awhile, consistent concepts emerged. Trial, error and client feedback allowed me to refine my ideas. I tested the concepts in the fire of my own life, with some spectacular results. One thing stood out: connecting with The Great Space, the Otherworld, the Cornucopia Reality, via the process of meditation, was fundamental to the process. So I took what I'd learned from my own experiences in the Cornucopia Reality and created a simple meditation process that anyone can use to become a conscious manifester. The Manifestation Matrix Meditation. And here's what I discovered: The Manifestation Matrix Meditation works.

I found that as I used The Manifestation Matrix Meditation, my creativity, my intuition and my ability to move forward in areas that would once have been terrifying for me all expanded rapidly. Since then, it has been even more fun to watch the life-transforming results my clients have experienced. You'll read some of their stories in this book.

But right now it's your turn. Let's dive in.

How to Perform Your Manifestation Matrix Meditation

Recall that The Manifestation Matrix, that field of consciousness, energy and matter you live in, is working all the time. Your thoughts, emotions, beliefs and behaviors are constantly transmitting energetic messages. Those energetic messages resonate with compatible frequencies which are then drawn into your experience (like attracts like). With your new awareness, you can begin to consciously direct that process.

Later I will walk you through the Five Steps of Conscious Manifestation in The Cornucopia Method of Manifestation. Underlying all of those steps, however, is the use of The Manifestation Matrix Meditation, which I'm about to show you. Sure, you can manifest consciously without The Manifestation Matrix Meditation just by following my five-step process; however, regular use of this meditation will make it much easier for you. So why not make it easy?

The Manifestation Matrix Meditation is a mindful walk through the chakras. It uses your intention and focus to run consciousness through all your energy centers. Regular use of this meditation will give you the ability to consciously move back and forth between the world of possibility (waves) and the world of matter (particles).

When you can do that, magic happens.

I have written out the meditation here for you to read. And I do recommend reading it through several times to understand how it works. Because the practice is most effective with your eyes closed, I have given you access to a free audio recording where I help you learn the meditation by walking you through it. Go to **www.kimberlyschneider.com/manifestationmatrixaudio** to download the audio if you haven't already done so. Then anytime you want to do the meditation, especially while you are learning it, just listen to The Manifestation Matrix Meditation on your mp3 player or computer (or burn it to a CD, whatever makes it more likely that you will use the meditation regularly).

Please don't practice the meditation while driving a car or multi-tasking, as the meditation does take you into an altered state of consciousness that is not conducive to other activities. Respect your practice, your safety and your abundance by setting aside the proper time and space to complete the experience properly. In this way, you'll reap the greatest benefits of the meditation.

A few final thoughts before you read on. As you begin to consciously bring your desires into your energy field, resistance will likely manifest at times. It may take the form of distracting thoughts, critical internal voices or feelings of discomfort in the body. Resistance is energy that is inconsistent with the frequency of your dreams. It can arise out of unconscious limiting beliefs, cellular memory or ancestral/collective material in your system. You don't need to figure out why it's there or where it is coming from.

When you notice resistance during your meditation time, rejoice!

You've been given an amazing opportunity to transform resistance in the moment. The easiest way to do this is to keep breathing. If your body is registering the resistance, just place a hand on that part of your body as you breathe. Notice the discomfort, the thoughts, the fears, the judgments, the worst case scenarios and the critical voices. Keep breathing. If the resistance appears as a thought form (a judgment, a to-do list, a belief) ask it: *"Where in my body do you live?"* and then place your hand on any place that registers a response.

You might also experience sadness, fear, anger or other challenging emotions. These emotions are coming up to be cleared, or in response to your process of saying *"Goodbye"* to who you have been. You do not need to do anything with the emotions but be a witness to your own process. Just keep breathing. Again, you can ask the emotion, *"Where in my body do you live?"* and then place your hand there. Continue to breathe, and direct feelings of acceptance and compassion to those parts of yourself. When in doubt about where to put your hand, try your heart, your abdomen or the top of your head (often I use two hands during this process). Then, leaving your hands in place and continuing to breathe, go back to where you left off in the meditation. You can move your hands throughout the meditation as resistance emerges in different places. Now that you know what to do with the resistance you don't need to worry about it.

You may or may not have experience meditating or sensing energy. Don't be concerned about that. You may sense, see or feel things during the meditation, or you may not. It will make no difference in the effectiveness of the meditation for you. **Intention is the key**. You don't need to be concerned about whether you have an intellectual understanding of anything I'll instruct you to do. Just know that it is happening as long as you intend it. Remember, energy follows intention. Thoughts create reality. Power follows practice. Just go with it. Try it and see how it works for you. Okay. On to The Manifestation Matrix Meditation!

These are the steps:

A. Ground Yourself
B. Awaken the Throne of Consciousness
C. Set Vibrational Goals
D. Give Voice to Your Dreams
E. Feel Your Bliss
F. Know What Is
G. Dance Your Desire into Being

H. Project Your Vibration
I. Fine-Tune Your Field with Gratitude

The Manifestation Matrix Meditation: A Simple, Proven Process for Manifesting Magic and Miracles

Get into a comfortable position. You can sit in a chair, sit on a meditation cushion or pillow on the floor, or lie down with your spine resting flat on the floor and a pillow under your knees. Some people even like to stand. If you find that you tend to fall asleep when meditating, you might want to sit or stand comfortably rather than lie down.

Close your eyes and focus on your breath. You don't need to change anything about your breathing; just notice it.

Bring to mind a manifestation goal, something that is near and dear to your heart. Let your goal expand so that it fills your entire energetic field. Allow your goal to vibrate with your field for a bit. Don't worry about how to do this. Just intend for it to happen.

As you do that, bring your awareness fully into your physical experience, into this body. Feel your body's contact with the chair, or with the floor, and allow your awareness to move into your root charka. Your root chakra extends from the edge of your tailbone toward the front of your body, through the perineal/genital region. Imagine a red ball of energy in your root chakra. It doesn't matter if you can see or feel this energy; just pretend that it is there.

Now let that ball become a cord and imagine that red cord of energy extending down and down through the furniture you're sitting on or lying on, down through the floor, through the structure of whatever building you're in, through the earth, through all the different layers of the earth, the asphalt, the dirt, the solids and liquids and gases; all the layers until you get to the very center of the earth, that molten fiery center of our planet. In whatever way makes sense to you, go ahead and attach a piece of this red cord to the center of the earth. You might imagine you are tying your cord to something in the center of the earth, or throwing an anchor down there. For some people, this process may take some doing. You might find yourself losing focus or having difficulty getting your energy anchored. Just stay with it.

When you have anchored your cord of energy to the center of the earth, allow your awareness to come back up that cord, bringing with it that vibrant energy, that grounded energy infused with life, coming up from the earth into the base of your spine. Allow that energy to very gently ease its way up your spine. As the energy moves up your back, it may or may not change color. Let the energy continue to move upward, all the way to the crown of your head.

This is the throne of your consciousness. The stepping-off point into the field of all possibilities. While you are here, spend a few moments focusing on your breath or your mantram. A mantram is a word or phrase that connotes the Holy Name, the ineffable. The Essence in all things. The particular word you choose is less important than what it represents for you. Let it be a word or phrase that holds a positive meaning or is at least neutral. Eknath Easwaran, the meditation teacher whose writings taught me about the mantram, recommends choosing an ancient name, one that has been used by many people over the centuries. For example, you might use Allah, Lord, Ave Maria, Jesus, Krishna or any of the countless names for the Holy One. The mantram I use is "I AM," which is a sacred phrase used in the Jewish, Christian and Hindu traditions. Feel free to borrow that if you don't have one of your own. Spend a minute or two, or as long as you like, silently in your mind repeating "I AM" or your own mantram. (I discuss mantram practice more fully in the chapter on Step V of The Cornucopia Method, Be Here Now. You can refer to that if you would like more explanation before you continue).

Now allow your manifestation goal to gently ease into that I AM space. Let the energy of it float in the throne of your consciousness. Let it crystallize and become a point of light that intersects with your own consciousness swimming in the All That Is.

Let your intention and awareness now move from your crown into the space just above and between your eyes. You can have a physical awareness of this place by looking up and in between your brows with your eyes closed. You might feel a sensation of tingling or movement in that area. Now extend your consciousness, still flowing down from your crown, out through this third-eye point as if it were a movie projector sending light out several inches in front of your forehead. Keeping your eyes closed, let your awareness focus on your manifestation goal once again. Allow that goal, infused with the energy of your crown and now running through your third eye, to begin projecting pictures in your mind. This may appear to you as visual images, which may be literal or symbolic. Or you might "see" sounds, or experience sensations, flashes of insight or a sense of knowing. Whatever form your "seeing" takes, allow this intersection of Pure Consciousness and your manifestation goal to provide a personal movie for you. If your mind wanders that's fine, just bring it back to your movie.

The images you experience may not seem to have any relationship to your original goal. And that's fine. Because what's important here is not the *form* your desire takes, or even the goal itself, but the energetic vibration your Essential Self was seeking when it put the goal into your mind. Just stay with the process. Stay with the energy.

As your inner movie continues to run, extend your awareness into your throat. This is your fifth chakra, the seat of your personal expression. Because sound brings energy into form, express the vibration of your movie through your voice with the sound of "Om" (rhymes with "home"). Om is an ancient sound containing an expression of your unity with the Absolute. It is also the sound of creation. Repeat the Om sound several times as your movie continues to run through your third eye. You have energy streaming through your crown, projecting out through your third eye and now flowing through your voice in the sound of Om. Feel your system resonate with the sacred sound.

Now allow your movie to be expressed through the sound of "Aaaaaaaaah." This sound is energetic power at the root of the word "amen." Amen means "so be it," or "let it be." It is an affirmation that what you are experiencing in your third eye already exists on some plane of reality. This is the energy of what Gregg Braden calls "the lost mode of prayer." It is a declaration of understanding that whatever you can conceive can be created through your connection with the All that Is. It is the basis for Jesus's statement, "Ask and it shall be given." Repeat the sound of "ah" several times. If you like, you may allow it to emerge as "ah-men."

Now that you are experiencing your connection to the Unified Field through the throne of your consciousness, seeing that connection expressed through your third eye and giving voice to your manifestation goal as it intersects with the Divine, bring your awareness down into your heart. Allow yourself to have the emotional experience, the feeling experience of that manifestation operating in your life right now, in this moment. Allow yourself to feel the joy, the ease, the freedom associated with your manifestation goal as it has been expressed through your inner movie and your voice. Let that emotional experience resonate in your physical body and notice how good that feels. Stay with this feeling for as long as you like.

From this place of joy, or whatever uplifting emotion you're experiencing, bring your awareness into your third chakra. This is the area between the bottom of your breastbone and the top of your belly button. It's the seat of your personal will and it's also that place where ego resides. Invite your ego onboard as a friend on this journey. The ego can only support the status quo. It can only align itself with what it knows. As you allow your ego to step into this new reality that you're already experiencing, seeing, speaking and feeling, the ego understands your manifestation goal as a present moment reality. It is right here, right now.

Knowing is beyond belief, faith, thinking or pretending. It is a state of existence that brooks no doubt, not because doubts are threatening, but because the state of knowing is so real that doubt does not occur to you. Let your Higher Self take the hand of your ego, so to speak. Allow yourself to know what you have experienced, seen, expressed and felt at every level of your being, down to every cell, down to the subatomic particles in your field.

Now bring your knowing into your second chakra, the pelvic region. This is where you dance that joyful reality into being through the physical expression of your body. Depending on where you are for this meditation, you can get up and move, or, if you prefer to remain lying or sitting, just move any part of your body. Roll your neck and shoulders, lift your arms or move in any way you wish. Let your physical movement act as your commitment to bring what you have experienced, seen, expressed, felt and known into the realm of action in the physical world.

Now bring the frequencies of all these experiences into your root chakra, that space near your tailbone that you awakened at the beginning of your meditation, and project these frequencies out from your root back down that cord of energy into the center of the earth, into the Ground Consciousness. Feel those frequencies pulsing through you, from your crown, through your third eye, through your throat, your heart, your solar plexus, your pelvis and now through your root into the center of the earth.

Draw your awareness back up that cord of energy again, from the Ground Consciousness into your body. As those frequencies re-enter your system, use your awareness and intention to refine them and bring them into closer alignment with what you saw in your movie. Again, don't worry about how to do this, just ask for it to happen. Continue to move the energy up and down your spine, into the earth and back up again. Each time bringing you closer and closer to complete resonance with your manifestation goal as it is expressed through your connection with Unity Consciousness.

Finally, send your awareness into the Ground Consciousness once more, back down that cord that extends from your root. As you do so, offer gratitude for the way the Ground Consciousness acts as a mirror, giving you feedback moment to moment to moment of exactly what frequencies you are sending out, giving you the perfect opportunity to consciously participate in this grand experiment of co-creation. The Christian mystic Meister Eckhart said, "If the only prayer you ever said was thank you, that would suffice." Indeed. Appreciation for where you are in this moment, for the miracle of being and for all the invisible energies that are, even now, clamoring to support your soul's desires — these are the foundations upon which a joyous life are built.

Take another deep breath now and very gently, knowing that you can return to this place at anytime, open your eyes.

A Quick Review of The Manifestation Matrix Meditation Process

A. Ground Yourself
B. Awaken the Throne of Consciousness
C. Set Vibrational Goals
D. Give Voice to Your Dreams
E. Feel Your Bliss
F. Know What Is
G. Dance Your Desire into Being
H. Project Your Vibration
I. Fine Tune Your Field with Gratitude

Part Two

The Cornucopia Method of Manifestation in Five Simple Steps

The Five Simple Steps of
The Cornucopia Method of Manifestation

The Cornucopia Method of Manifestation is designed to help you create your reality more mindfully. It is a clear and simple method for conscious manifestation.

The Five Steps of The Cornucopia Method of Manifestation are:

I.   Decide
II. Know Yourself
III. Befriend Your Body
IV. Raise Your Vibrational Frequency and
V.   Be Here Now

Part Two of this book will explain what each of the five steps means, give you some insights into how to do the steps and also offer you examples and exercises so the process will be meaningful for you.

It may take you some time to digest all the material in this section. Read, reflect, do the available exercises, reflect some more and then re-read where necessary. Remember, this isn't just a book you've picked up to read once and put away. You can use it as a complete home study course, a tool for creating the life you want to be living.

You will enhance your ability to integrate the material and apply it to your life right away *if* you practice The Manifestation Matrix Meditation on a regular basis. So if you've skipped Part One to jump right into the meat of the book, you've missed something critical. Go back and pick up that piece or use The Manifestation Matrix audio to guide you through the process.

Once you have integrated the five steps, you'll be able to walk yourself through them quickly whenever you need them. Keep in mind, however, that while your ability to consciously manifest will grow better and better, you may not perfect it during this lifetime. (But hey, you just might —

I certainly haven't reached the pinnacle, but who am I to put limits on YOU...)

The point is this: it's natural to make progress and then feel like you're going backwards. When you catch yourself falling into old patterns, just know that's part of the process. That's the material for your practice.

And we all have blind spots, too. Even the masters and the mavens. So above all, be gentle with yourself. The more compassionate you are with yourself and others as you work with these concepts, the easier the entire process will be for you. Your greatest ally may be your ability to laugh at your ego's attempts to hijack your evolution of consciousness.

Reality is all an illusion anyway, remember? A wondrous, beautiful, magnificent and occasionally baffling illusion. We are all pieces of Essence, dancing through this ever-expanding experiment in materiality. And we're all doing the best we can with the resources and experience we have in any given moment.

So *Namaste!* (Sanskrit for "the Divine in me bows to the Divine in you.") Have some fun with this.

The Cornucopia Method of Manifestation Step I: Decide

The first step in conscious manifestation is to decide you are a conscious manifester.

That is, you need to recognize yourself as a participator in creation. You must accept that everything you need to learn and know is contained in the day-to-day happenings of your life, because you are the one who created those happenings (whether you like them or not).

The First Decision: Responsibility

If you want to manifest consciously, you must accept complete responsibility for your entire life: for your level of consciousness, your thoughts and beliefs, your words, emotions, feelings, behaviors and results. It doesn't matter whether you know HOW you brought a particular experience into your life; until you are willing to accept complete responsibility for it, you won't be able to change it.

To be clear, I'm not suggesting that other people have no influence on how you feel or what happens to you. We are all participating in this same energetic soup, and somebody else's spice is definitely going to impact the taste of your sugar (and vice versa). If you are having an experience, however, it's because you either determined at a soul level that you wanted/needed exactly this sort of experience for your soul's benefit, or you have otherwise called it into your life via your energetic vibration since your arrival. End of story.

As long as you refuse responsibility for your happiness, your suffering, your successes and failures, you are helpless to create the life you really want. And what's more, if you won't take charge of your own power, I can guarantee someone else will be glad to direct it for you. Anyone who doesn't know how to access the Unified Field to get the energy they need is on a constant search to get it from somewhere else. You don't need to be the place they go to fill up.

Not everyone who subverts your life force will do it with negative intentions. Often the energetic exchange is unconscious. Children are great examples of this. When children are young, after all, they are designed to be self-centered—it's up to you as an adult to help the children in your life learn where their energy stops and yours begins. And there are likely many other people you've surrendered your power to, whether or not they've asked you to do it: partners, parents, friends and colleagues.

But another person's motive for draining your life force doesn't really matter. The result is the same: less energy for you to realize your own potential.

In case you're thinking that surrendering your own power for the sake of someone else's goals is a worthy cause, think again. When people get where they're going by stealing power from others, they might achieve some ego-driven goals but they'll never realize their full potential either. They'll never experience their reason for being. (In my experience, in order to find their reason for being they would need to somehow find their own connection to the Unified Field—although they may certainly call it something else.) So giving your power away to someone who hasn't found their own path to Essence is like giving junk food to someone whose body is starved for fresh, whole nutrition.

How do you know when you've given your power away? When your soul feels restless, when nothing satisfies you, when you know that there must be more to life than this... those are clues.

You may think it's someone else's fault you've never: climbed a mountain; eaten at a sidewalk bistro in Paris; written your book; belly-danced at the Renaissance Fair; started your own business; pursued the longing to paint, sculpt or sing just for the pure pleasure of creating...or whatever it is that your heart longs to experience. You may secretly believe that if it weren't for your obligations, you'd have a more marvelous existence.

When you've given your power away, you might believe that other people's needs or outside circumstances trap you in an undesirable life (a life that, in truth, you have chosen for yourself).

I have certainly fallen prey to this pattern. At various times I told myself:

I couldn't explore alternative spiritual practices because my husband might freak out (he did; we survived and we're both better for it);

I couldn't leave a good-paying job to pursue my passions because my daughter might have another heart surgery;

I couldn't travel without my kids.

These are just a few of the stories I made up-convenient ways to avoid the scary and shocking truth that I was in charge of my own life and only I could create the happiness I might find in expressing my Essential Self.

There's a psychological concept called projection that means we see in others, or attribute to others, those parts of ourselves we aren't comfortable owning. Personal power is one of the most common projections. We push our power onto other people, circumstances or institutions and then pretend we don't have choices about our lives.

The surest way to discover where you are giving your power away is to notice your resentments. Take a moment now and think of three things or people you resent. Are your kids draining your energy? Maybe you need to drop the idea that you should be available to them all the time. Does your partner seem to be stifling you? What stories have you made up about what he or she would do if you acted on your secret dreams? Is your best friend driving you to distraction with stories of her vacations? Perhaps you need to re-think the belief that you can't travel where you long to go.

How does it serve you to deny your own power? Maybe you're afraid you'll do what you think you want, and still not be happy. Or that you won't be loved or admired if you step out of the roles you've been playing. Or that you'll let go of your masks and find nothing inside. Be honest with yourself. While it may be true that you'll meet some resistance when you behave differently than people expect, whatever it is that keeps you from consciously creating your life, it's yours. Your fears. Your hesitation. Your own limiting beliefs.

Own them, and your life will transform.

How can you take your projections back? You can quit blaming others for making your life smaller than you know it can be. You can reclaim your power. You can commit to taking 100% responsibility for your level of consciousness, your thoughts, your words, your emotions, your feelings, your behaviors and your results.

I'm not going to lie to you. Deciding to take complete responsibility for your own life story is scary. The process of taking back your power projections will stretch you. People you know may be shaken, angry, confused, excited, awed or frightened when you stand in your creative power. Some may even leave. But the relationships that remain will be cleaner, clearer and freer. Perhaps you will actually inspire someone you love to follow her or his dreams. More importantly, you will now be free to realize your own true desires.

Essential Self and Ego

But what desires are true desires? How do you distinguish goals, which, once achieved, will leave you feeling hollow, from activities that are in alignment with your soul's purpose?

The answer to these questions lies in the distinction between the ego and the Essential Self. To explore these concepts, let's take a journey back to before you came into your body. Imagine yourself there in the Unified Field once upon a time when:

In a time beyond time, in a space beyond space also known as the Unified Field, Essence pulses with a desire to experience itself. Out of that desire emerges an Essential Self. This Essential Self understands its function as a unique expression of Essence – a timeless entity contemplating its entry (or re-entry) into the space-time continuum.

Essential Self reviews the record of its relationship to material reality and considers what new experiences might produce the best opportunities for expansion. This knowledge gives rise to an energetic blueprint for your incarnation. The energetic blueprint is not a predetermined course of events, but more like a carefully selected list of ingredients from which your entire system will be able to draw upon throughout your life.

Pulsing with the ever-amplifying desire for experience, Essential Self watches the multiple billions of possibilities that might arise from this new study in form. Holding an image of your highest potential, your Essential Self rides a wave of possibility all the way into the Ground Consciousness of Earth. And Ground Consciousness responds with a new creation: your physical form. And now you are in it.

Although every cell in your new form dances with the song of your Essential Self, the song is difficult to single out in the midst of all the competing input. Form! What an amazing experience! Sounds, tastes, sights, sensations and smells! Out of this amorphous soup of stimuli, your system must create an individualized consciousness to sort out and make sense of all the information – some part that can comprehend itself as a separate character and play out its stories in this grand theatre of experience.

*So Essential Self nurtures the development of an **ego: a construct of the mind that works to support the illusion of your separation from Essence.** The ego thinks you are only your personality or body. Your ego's fantasy that you are cut off from Essence (or the ego's failure to appreciate that Essence exists at all) is a necessary fiction. It allows Essence to fully engage in material experience.*

Your Essential Self is aware of your ego. It appreciates the function your ego serves. However, the feeling is not mutual. Neither is the awareness. Your ego has no comprehension of your Essential Self. Ego believes it is essentially alone in the universe.

As your life unfolds, your Essential Self, your ego and your physical form interact with the collective vibrations contained in your immediate environment, your accumulated experiences, your ancestral history (in your DNA) and your culture. Most of these vibrations originate outside of your ego's awareness. This intersection of energies transmits a vibratory message to the Ground Consciousness. Ground Consciousness responds with a storyline made up of elements drawn from your energetic blueprint.

Since your ego originated with your physical form, it wasn't involved in the plans your Essential Self made for its sojourn into materiality. Therefore, some of the experiences emerging from Ground Consciousness are baffling to the ego. When ego encounters a situation that challenges its perception of how things should be, it responds with resistance.

The ego's desires arise out of its attempts to preserve the reality it has created based upon its fantasy of separation from Essence.

Authentic Desires, on the other hand, arise out of your connection with Essence. They are expressed through your Essential Self. These desires may take on a material form (because you are living in a material world), yet they are expressions of intangible qualities that express who you really are. These qualities include: Security, Creativity, Connection, Power from Within (Power that emanates from a connection to Essence), Love, Beauty, Expression, Creative Intelligence, Intellectual Stimulation, Understanding, Clarity of Vision, Freedom, Boundlessness, Peace and Joy.

So, as you decide to take responsibility for your life, remember that your ego won't recognize the efforts of your Essential Self to fulfill your happiness. When you use the lens of the ego to create stories about your life, you will feel frustrated, angry and confused. However, if you trust in the wisdom of your Essential Self, you will understand that events your ego interprets as punishments, or problems or evidence that you've done something wrong, are actually opportunities to take you closer to your Authentic Desires.

Authentic Desires and Ego Desires

Authentic Desires arise from your Essential Self. They are big- picture desires, and they are not attached to form. In other words, there is no limit to the number of ways in which an Authentic Desire can be realized, or the variety of forms through which an Authentic Desire can be made manifest. In contrast, Ego Desires come from the part of you that lives in the illusion of separation, so they are limited in perspective.

You experience suffering when your ego decides that its desires cannot be realized. But you don't need to eradicate your Ego Desires or feel badly that you have them. In fact, your Ego Desires hint at your Authentic Desires; you can use them to point the way back to your Essential Self. You can even integrate, or weave together, your Ego Desires and Authentic Desires so that they work together to create your reality. (And, incidentally, integrating your ego is much more effective than attempting to destroy it. There is no point in supporting the illusions of separation and internal conflict when you can have every aspect of who you are working to support your soul's intentions.)

So how do you identify Ego Desires? What allows you to distinguish them from Authentic Desires? And what does it take to integrate the two? To illustrate, let's look at the example of Jane. Jane has worked for the same company for over ten years. She enjoys her job and makes a good living. Then Jane's employer merges with another company. Her department, and her job, are eliminated. Jane has no job. Naturally Jane is frustrated, angry and, most of all, frightened. The future is uncertain. Jobs in her industry are scarce and her city has just been flooded with highly qualified applicants in her field who are looking for work due to the merger. Jane feels panicked. She feels she must find another job. Immediately.

Jane does all the right things she's learned to do to obtain a new position. She updates her resume and calls everyone she knows to tell them she's looking for work. She joins networking organizations and schedules informational interviews. But no offers emerge. In fact, in most cases she doesn't even get a response to the letters and resumes she sends.

Jane wants a new job. She believes she needs a new job since her bank account is nearly depleted. She does not have enough money to make her next mortgage payment.

Is Jane's desire for a new job an Ego Desire, or an Authentic Desire?

First we must ask: what are the deeper desires beneath Jane's longing for a new job? Jane wants to feel secure. She wants to make a meaningful contribution in the world. She wants to express her gifts and be connected to other people who are united in a common purpose. She wants to fulfill her commitments. Each one of these desires is an Authentic Desire, *which may or may not take the form of a new job.*

Jane's attachment to obtaining any particular job would be an Ego Desire. However, by looking more deeply, we can see that Jane's Ego Desire of a new job points to her Authentic Desires. And she can integrate her Ego Desires and Authentic Desires by consciously tapping into her longing for security, creative expression, connection and purpose each day and then acting on the inspiration she receives. Do you see the difference? If Jane views her life through her Ego Desires, her options are limited and she will be living in a state of panic and fear. Even if she finds another job, the fear and panic will not completely subside, because now her ego knows that security in the form of a job is just an illusion. If, however, Jane can act from a larger perspective, there is no limit to how her desires might be fulfilled.

Jane may end up launching a new business. She may declare bankruptcy and emerge stronger than ever. She may have money come to her in unexpected and marvelous ways. She may even get a job. But the job she gets will be one that she attracts through her connection with her Essential Self.

What will be critical for Jane as she moves through this process is to release her resistance to whatever form is emerging and to return, again and again, to her Authentic Desires. If Jane can trust that her Authentic Desires are being realized regardless of what her external circumstances may present to her, she will release her resistance and bring herself into alignment with her Essential Self. She will gain what St. Paul calls "the peace that passes understanding" and the Bhagavad Gita refers to as "the peace in which all sorrows end." And from that place—the place of connection with Source—Jane can manifest anything.

Of course, when you are being presented with a situation your ego hates, it can be challenging to shift your awareness into your Authentic Desires. When you are frightened, angry or confused, it is easy to get caught in a story of "this shouldn't be happening," or "I'm doing something wrong."

If, at this point, you're wondering exactly how to release resistance so you can move into your Authentic Desires, don't worry. The tools you need are here for you. In fact, I'm going to show you an exercise that will help later in this chapter. And that's just a start. I'll give you lots of different ways to let go of resistance and release attachment to form throughout this book. For now, just consider the possibility that there's nothing wrong with whatever is happening in your life. Then, even if you feel confused, stick with the process and observe the results over time. Remember, this material can create big changes in your life—if you commit to reading the book all the way through once and then going back through to work the exercises. Because if you can notice your stories, let them go and adopt an attitude of trust, you will be stepping into the realm of magic and miracles.

I have Ego Desires, just like anyone else. Each moment is an invitation to notice my ego's stories and wishes and allow them to lead me to my Authentic Desires. To release attachment to form. Some situations are easier than others. One of the most challenging situations for me happened around our daughter Bridget's birth.

A Perfect Birth

It was a warm day in June and I was thirty-five weeks pregnant. I was looking forward to a natural and easy childbirth this time; with our first baby I'd had four and a half days of labor followed by a C-section. I had a detailed birth plan that I'd reviewed with my obstetrician about what I wanted my hospital experience to look like. I'd also been working with a counselor who specialized in prenatal psychology, and she'd created meditations to support me in a textbook for easy delivery without drugs or medical interventions. We didn't plan to have any more children, and I really wanted the experience of a natural birth.

I knew I had several weeks before the baby (whom we had already named Bridget) would arrive, but that morning I had a burst of energy and a day off of work so I decided to go pick up some of the things I would need before she was born. I was lumbering through the parking lot at Target, a protective hand supporting my swollen abdomen as I stepped up from the curb, when I heard someone say, "When are you due?"

I looked up to see a scrawny white woman with limp, straw-colored hair leaning against the building. A burning cigarette dangled from her fingers. Her clothes seemed to hang off of her; even her red employee vest looked two sizes too large. She peered at me over the glasses perched on her nose. "Not for another month," I replied, managing a smile. She lifted the cigarette to her mouth and took a long, deep breath, then slowly looked me up and down as she blew smoke out of her wrinkled lips.

As I stepped through the automatic doors into the air-conditioned store I heard her laughing softly behind me. "Wanna make a bet, honey?"

I felt a surge of irritation. How rude! Yes, I was a little big for eight months. Okay — I was huge. Still, I was astonished and insulted that a perfect stranger felt free to comment on the state of my body.

I pulled out my list of baby items and took a deep breath. Back to the task at hand. I wasn't going to let that woman ruin my mood.

The rest of the day was a flurry of activity. After my errands I brought Maddie, our four-year old, home from school, cleaned the house and cooked dinner. That evening I did my birth meditation and wrote in my pregnancy journal before I went to bed.

Around 4:00 a.m. the next morning, an unsettling dream interrupted my sleep. I opened my eyes and lay in the dark. With my hands on my belly, I counted the baby's movements, going over the details of the dream in my mind. I'd been sitting in a doctor's office with an obstetrician. She looked me in the eyes, held my hands and told me, "You're going to have an emergency C-section. Your baby needs to be born today."

I got out of bed and wandered into the room we'd prepared for Bridget. I gazed at her crib and then took a seat in the rocking chair, thinking about how much I wanted a natural childbirth. This was it. This was my last chance to have that experience. But what if I really did need a C-section? And what if Bridget needed to be born today? Was my dream a message? Or was it just a way of processing my fears?

I considered ignoring the dream, because it was not telling me what I wanted to hear. I wanted a natural birth. I didn't want complications. And I certainly didn't want an emergency C-section. I had been doing everything right to create a natural birth experience.

But I continued counting movements and realized that while Bridget was moving, she did not seem as active as she'd been the day before. Yes, I wanted a natural birth, but that was because a natural birth was what I thought was good for the baby. That's what I really wanted: whatever was best for her.

I couldn't go back to sleep. So I went into the office to finish up some work, just in case. After all, the dream seemed to confirm the words of the lady in the Target parking lot. Was she some sort of suburban oracle? I hoped not.

By 6:00 a.m. I was at my desk, finishing up a memo about all my pending projects. At 8:30 I called the doctor's office and asked to come in, explaining that the baby wasn't moving as much as usual. He said, "Come on in. That's why we have the equipment here."

At the doctor's office I had several tests to check on the baby's condition. As I lay there, Bridget became much more active. I started feeling silly. Had I really come there just because I had a dream that I needed a C-section? Maybe I should have stayed home, put my feet up and counted movements.

Finally the nurse told me to go wait in the lobby while the doctor looked over all the results. I was getting hungry so I said, "Okay, I'll be right back, I'm just going to grab a snack."

"Um, why don't you just wait please," the nurse said. "I'm sure the doctor will be right with you."

Sure enough, a few minutes later, my doctor came into the lobby and sat down next to me. He smiled and said, "I want you to take a deep breath, okay?"

"All right. What's up?"

"Do you see that wheelchair over there?" he pointed. "That's for you. Your baby's in distress. It's noon right now. I'm taking you to a hospital room for prep. Call anyone you want to be here, because you need to be in the operating room by 2:00 p.m. This baby needs to be born today."

As the doctor wheeled me to the hospital, I was feeling an assortment of competing emotions: fear for the baby, sadness that I wasn't going to have the birth I'd planned, but mostly relief that I'd listened to the signs I'd received. I wondered what my doctor would make of it all.

"You know why I really came in today? I had a dream that I needed an emergency C-section." The doctor was silent for a few moments. Then he said, "That actually doesn't surprise me at all. Mothers usually know. I'm glad you are here."

Bridget was born at 2:17 p.m. She needed oxygen and support in the special care nursery. It would be months before we would find out about her heart defect and developmental delays, but one thing was clear already: she needed extra help beyond what my body was able to provide her. My doctor later told us that if I had not come in that day, Bridget would have died before her birth.

My Ego Desires around Bridget's arrival in the world took the form of a natural birth, at the time she was due. They did not include an emergency C-section before my doula could arrive to support me, or a premature baby who was too weak to nurse. But if I had remained attached to my ego's desires [Ego Desires?], there would have been no space for Bridget in my life. Bridget has some extraordinary needs. I would not have been able to mother her adequately without a correspondingly extraordinary deepening of my intuition — and of my faith. Her unusual birth was a perfect vehicle to initiate us into our journey together.

I made a choice to take responsibility for co-creating my experience. I let go of my ego's stories about what was happening and opened up to a larger perspective. I trusted that perhaps my Essential Self knew some things my ego did not.

When you see and accept your ego's resistance, when you make a conscious decision to be present to what *is* rather than how you think things *should be*, you begin the process of integrating your ego and your Essential Self. When that happens, you have all the facets of who you are working together, rather than at cross purposes. Your life will be easier, and you will get the results you want more quickly. You will have regular experiences of intense satisfaction as you realize dreams that hold the vibration of your highest intentions for yourself. Regular practice of The Manifestation Matrix Meditation will help you with this process.

Your Essential Self understands and has compassion for the ego and its desires. And as long as you recognize the ego for what it is (a tool designed to support you while you reside in physical form), you can allow ego to offer input without leaving your ego in charge. You won't be fooled into thinking that your ego is YOU.

The goal of this book is to help you experience and enjoy your Authentic Desires *within the context of a material experience*. You can appreciate the intangible qualities inherent in your Authentic Desires while also appreciating the physical experience. You can know yourself as Essence and as an individual human person in a material experience *at the same time*. Material reality gives you a fantastic canvas on which to view your Essential creativity.

Regular practice of The Manifestation Matrix Meditation will naturally allow your Authentic Desires to move to the forefront of your consciousness. Ego Desires will, of course, continue to arise but your practice will make it easier to recognize them for what they are and address them. They will no longer run your life and create your reality!

The Second Decision: Set an Intention

Now that you've accepted your role as a conscious manifester, it's time to ask yourself: what do I want to dream into being? After all, if you are creating your reality momenttomoment, why not make a conscious decision about how you'd like things to be?

Napoleon Hill, author of *Think and Grow Rich*, spent years studying and cataloguing the characteristics of wildly successful people. He found that they had multiple characteristics in common. Two stood out as the most important:

• A clear and definite purpose partnered with

• A burning desire to realize that purpose

Why is the burning desire so important? Because you are constantly interacting with the desires and manifestations of other individuals, as well as the collective unconscious of your family and culture. Unless you are clear about how you want to focus your awareness, your energy will be used in a way that may not serve you. Motivational speaker and business coach Lee Milteer, author of *Spiritual Power Tools*, puts it this way: if you haven't engaged your life force to achieve your own goals, another person will pirate it to service their own agenda. Or, as shaman Alberto Villoldo suggests in his book, *Courageous Dreaming*, if you're not courageously dreaming, you'll get caught in someone else's nightmare. That's pretty serious, isn't it?

What if you don't have a burning desire? What if you have no idea what you want to do with your life?

I'm going to go out on a limb here. I'll bet that, no matter who you are or what your experiences have been, you do have a dream somewhere inside you and the passion to match it. It's just been buried for so long you've forgotten what it is. But no worries. By the time you finish this book you'll be on the way to resurrecting your dreams. And if

69

you already know what dreams you want to realize, I can help you get there more quickly, having fun along the way.

EXERCISE:

Here's a multi-part exercise to get you started on the journey of possibility; grab your journal and read on:

1. Life Purpose
Your life purpose is dynamic — you will likely not define it the same way over decades. So don't worry that you'll be stuck forever with whatever you write here. It's your life! Figure out your purpose as you go. At the moment, you may have no clue about your life purpose. If you don't, that's okay. Just skip to the next question and you can come back to this after you finish the section on Step II: Know Yourself.

My life purpose, as I understand it to be at the moment, is:

(write the entire sentence and then complete it in your journal)

For example, as I'm writing this book, I recognize my own life purpose to be raising the vibration of planet Earth by helping create as many conscious manifesters as I can. I've heard Deepak Chopra identify his life purpose as making other people happy. I would guess that Oprah Winfrey's life purpose is to help other people live their best lives.

You'll know you're playing in the arena of life purpose when thinking about it makes you feel joyful, enthusiastic, energized and peaceful at the same time. When you think about living in the flow of your life purpose, you are happy to be alive. You feel grateful. You have a passion for being. (Not at every moment of your life, perhaps, but in general).

Again, if you aren't yet in touch with your life purpose, that's fine. Your life is a grand experiment. You'll get it figured out.

2. Current Manifestation Intention

Your current intention is a focused desire that you want to manifest in your life. Of course, you have lots of intentions, small to large. For this exercise, please pick just one, ideally the one that has the most charge, excitement and energy around it. *Please note: whether or not you have any idea of HOW you might manifest this intention is COMPLETELY IRRELEVANT to this exercise. This is not the time for a plan of action!* (*Save that for later*). You will likely get clarity around your present manifestation intention as you continue working with The Manifestation Matrix Meditation. (If you haven't started that practice, now would be a good time!) Just pick something that appeals to you, whether it seems realistic or not. For instance, my intention at this moment is to create the most useful, effective and transformational book I can write. That's my focus as I'm working. I have other intentions regarding health for my family, time and travel with my husband and kids and living part-time in western Ireland. If I were working through this book, I'd pick one of those to focus on. Your intention for right now might even be something like: *I want to manifest clarity of purpose around my life's work"* or *I want to remember what engages my passions.* Just pick something that works for you.

My intention for conscious manifestation is: (**write in your journal**)

This dream is important to me because: (**write in your journal**)

71

The second question above engages the burning desire. What is your passionate WHY? Again, if you aren't completely clear on this yet, it will emerge as you go. Just work with where you are at this moment.

Now take another look at what you wrote for the previous two statements. Notice if you've written anything in terms of what you don't want, i.e. *I don't want to be lonely* or *I am tired of feeling fat* or *I am afraid I won't have the tuition for my kids' school next year.* If you've written your intentions in the negative, congratulations. Sometimes you have to know what you don't want to figure out what you do want. Now rewrite your intentions in a positive light. For example: *I want to have the resources to send my kids to the best school for them because it will feel fantastic to support them in that way.* Or *I want to find and maintain my ideal weight because it feels great to be healthy and strong and feel happy and grateful when I look in the mirror. Or I want to find the perfect life partner so that I can feel contentment and companionship while sharing my love and life with someone.* You get the idea.

Finally, read back through all of your answers again. Rewrite your intention as if it is happening right now. Include your sense of gratitude that this wonderful experience is happening for you in this moment.

Here's an example:

I am so happy and grateful now that my book, Everything You Need Is Right Here, is selling so well! I'm excited knowing that the ideas, which have worked for me and for my clients, are now being discovered by a larger audience. We are creating a critical mass of conscious manifesters and miracle makers all over the planet. Every month I am meeting delighted people who are successfully using the concepts I'm sharing to illuminate their own life purpose. Together we are envisioning and bringing into form an enlightened world. We are enjoying an environment where peace, creativity, abundance and love abound. Each new seeming challenge for our planet and our species calls out the best in us, and we delight in being at the cutting-edge of our evolution. It is so much fun to learn and grow and unite our capabilities as expressions of Essence with our experiences in these wonderful physical forms. What an amazing time to be alive!

That was my present intention, of course. Yours will be unique to you. And let me be the first to give you permission to intend something material, something just for you, if that makes your heart sing. I found for myself that my true purpose did not emerge until I became comfortable with focusing on what I wanted for myself on a material level. So if it's your own private jet to take you wherever you want to go in the world, or a beautiful home in exactly the right environment or singing on Broadway, that's okay. Go for it. Remember to start with (and my thanks to Bob Proctor for this insight) *I am so happy and grateful now that...* (Are you starting to think that a Conscious Manifestation journal might be a handy thing to have?)

My intention for conscious manifestation is: **(write the entire sentence in your journal)**

3. Vibrational Goal Setting
Look at the paragraph(s) you previously wrote to represent your current manifestation intention. Can you identify the intangible qualities expressed in your intention? Identifying which intangible qualities are operating in your intentions will help you later in your manifestation process. To refresh your memory, intangible qualities are states of being that arise out of your connection with Essence. I've listed some examples below. Perhaps you will come up with some I have not identified.

Intangible Qualities: Security, Creativity, Relationship, Power from Within (Power that emanates from a connection to Essence), Love, Unity, Beauty, Expression, Creative Intelligence, Intellectual Stimulation, Understanding, Clarity of Vision, Freedom, Boundlessness, Peace and Joy.

Note: Identifying the intangible or energetic qualities your Essential Self is seeking is the most important part of this exercise. As you move through life, the *form* your goal takes will likely change over time. Please don't confuse Essence with any temporary form it might take.

So, for instance, if your manifestation goal is a better relationship with your life partner, the intangibles you desire might be love, connection, partnership, being seen and appreciated for you who are. Your Essential Self is seeking those intangible experiences — and they are actually *already available to you, right here, right now.* Those intangible experiences may or may not express themselves in the form of your current relationship. They might, instead, be found in learning to connect with yourself. Or noticing all the ways you experience love, partnership and being seen in other aspects of your life. And — here's the challenge — as long as you are trying to force any one relationship to be the source of those experiences, you will likely not find them there. Because no particular situation, relationship or form is actually the source of the intangibles. The Source is the source. Essence is the source.

At this point, your ego might be saying, "Hey, wait a minute. I'm reading this book because I want to manifest my goals. Now you're telling me to just be happy with whatever I get? That I'm supposed to forget about having what I want and settle for something less?"

Don't worry. I'm not suggesting, nor would I ever suggest, that you settle for anything less than what your soul really desires. The paradox is, that as long as you are attached to your desire manifesting in a particular way, you can block it from happening. Not only that, but being attached to outcome and form often makes you miss an experience much more satisfying, or even spectacular, than your ego could come up with on its own.

I have witnessed clients manifesting wondrous events in their lives on countless occasions, when they finally let go of trying to direct the outcome. One client, Brendan, came to me for a Manifestation Matrix reading, where we looked at

74

the archetypes and energies at each of his chakras to help him get clarity on where his energy was stuck and what actions he might take to shift his life experiences. Brendan was seriously unhappy in his job. The reading suggested that a change of environment would serve him, but more importantly, a change in attitude. If Brendan did not expand his ideas about what was possible for him, he would just take his thought patterns into the next work situation and recreate the experiences he was now having.

At first, Brendan was resistant to the idea that he could leave. He was a computer programmer and he was not trained in the newest languages companies were requiring of their employees. Not only that, but he lived in a rural area and drove an hour each way to work. His current job allowed him to do some work from home and commute just three days per week. Brendan was certain that even if he somehow found another job, the company would require him to make the drive into the city five days per week, which was not a good option for his family.

Brendan and I discussed how his stories were keeping him in a difficult situation. After all, as author Richard Bach reminds us, "argue for your limitations, and sure enough, they're yours!" I invited Brendan to let go of HOW he might end up getting what he wanted, or exactly what it would look like, and focus instead on how it would feel to be in a job where he felt appreciated, enjoyed his work and had an easy commute. "An easy commute!" Brendan exclaimed. "That's not possible. This is a small town. There won't be anything like that around here." Brendan caught himself then and started laughing. "Okay, I know what you're going to say. Forget about the how. Focus on my intention." Brendan made a commitment then and there to work the steps of The Cornucopia Method and keep coming back to how he wanted to feel rather than focusing on how unhappy his work situation was or how impossible it was to find something else.

A couple of months later I heard from Brendan. "You're not going to believe this," he said. "Or, maybe *you* will believe it. I got a new job! They are going to teach me the programming language I wanted to learn, the owners are fantastic people, they are paying me well and—here's the amazing part—the office is a few minutes from my house! I've never even heard of the place and it's right in my hometown."

Another client, Sara, had bought my home study course and was in a year-long intensive coaching program with me. She had come to me to work on her business, but during one session her daughter was uppermost in her mind. Cathy was moving across the country for college. Sara loved the school but wished it were easier to get to from home. "I'd feel so much better if she just had some family in town. Someone who could be there in case of emergency, and a place she could go sometimes for Shabbat or to celebrate holidays away from home." We talked about visioning Cathy thriving in her new environment, finding a supportive community that would make her feel at home and ease Sara's concerns about her being so far away.

Several weeks later Cathy had started school. Everything was going smoothly, but there was a mix-up in her prescription medication and she asked Sara if she could please call the pharmacy near the campus to get it straightened out. Sara picked up the phone and called California. She reached the pharmacist and gave her daughter's name and address in St. Louis. "Wow, that's really close to where I grew up!" the pharmacist said. "Where did you go to high school?" It turned out that she and Sara knew many of the same people. In fact, Sara soon discovered that the pharmacist was actually a younger cousin she'd never met. They were soon making plans for Cathy to go over to Sara's cousin's for dinner, which she has now done many times. Sara manifested family in Cathy's college town, a family member she did not even know existed prior to their synchronistic phone conversation! "I finally get it now," Sara reflected. "I am beginning to understand how this manifestation stuff works. I never could have orchestrated that in a million years. I just had to let go and trust that Cathy would be okay. And look what happened!"

The purpose of having and focusing on a manifestation goal is only *to put you into a feeling state that connects you with Essence.* Form is one of the five major illusions we experience in this life, along with Separation, Time, Duality and Control (that's the subject of my next book). That's why releasing attachment to outcome, or form, is a critical aspect of conscious manifestation. Form is not the real object of any desire that arises from your Essential Self.

This is the difference between what a lot of self-improvement teachers call visualization and what we'll call Vibrational Goal Setting. Visualization and goal setting can create confusion unless you first distinguish between the ego (the part that wants to control the HOW and the WHAT) and the Essential Self (the part that knows *you already are and always will be connected to your Source*...and can lead your conscious mind right back to that place of connection and bliss). The way to do that is to identify the intangibles. The intangibles allow you to stop focusing on the form and bring your energy and attention to the energy beneath.

What intangibles did you identify in your manifestation intention? To help you understand how this works, I can point out the intangibles in mine. As I read through the intention I wrote, I can identify these intangibles:

- o *Intellectual Stimulation* (ideas);
- o *Creativity* (creating conscious manifesters);
- o *Connection* (meeting people);
- o *Public Impact* (touching many people);
- o Igniting *Happiness* in others (people being delighted with their results);
- o *Community* (playing together with others to create a new world);
- o *Innovation* (cutting-edge); and
- o *Raising the Vibration of the Planet* (pretty self explanatory).

77

Now, you try it. Go back to your own manifestation intention and identify the intangibles that jump out at you. Write them in your journal, next to your intention.

4. Letting Go

We've identified the importance of letting go, releasing attachment to form and outcome. The ego doesn't like to do this. It wants to maintain the illusion of control. So you must teach your ego to surrender to something bigger than itself.

You might call it God/dess.

You might call it Essence.

The Absolute.

The Vessel that Holds the Ever Expanding Multi-Verse....(you get the idea).

But how to do it?
A few tools I use to help me let go are:

Chanting...especially in an ancient language my ego can't engage – such as Sanskrit, Aramaic, Hebrew, Latin or Irish

Focusing on the breath

Silently repeating a mantram...one of the Holy Names

Another important aspect of letting go is bringing the body into the process. You are a physical being, and your blood and bone, your tissues and cells (and the spaces between the cells) are holding the memory of your attachment to outcome and form. You've got to work with them. Let your heart, that magnificent transmitter of love and energy, speak to your mind. Dance with your craving. Run with your anger. Breathe through uncertainty. Engage in heart-opening yoga exercises to deal with your grief.

And if you want a tried and true exercise that engages your body but is unobtrusive enough to use anytime, anywhere, on the go, I've created an audio that explains and leads you through my very favorite letting-go exercise. It's my gift to you—you can access it for free at **www.KimberlySchneider.com/lettinggoaudio**. I'd be delighted to hear how it works for you.

The Next Step

Congratulations! Now that you've decided to take responsibility for your life and named your present intention for manifestation (including the intangible aspects of your authentic desire) you are ready for Conscious Manifestation Step II: Know Yourself.

The section covering Step II of The Cornucopia Method of Manifestation is longer and a bit more complex—because YOU are a complex being! Knowing yourself is a big task, and worth every ounce of effort it takes. It's what you came here for, remember? You are Essence having a material experience. Your life arose out of Essence's desire to know itself as itself.

Knowing yourself is a life-long process and many great thinkers have written entire treatises on this one topic. But I'm going to make it easier for you. I'll be giving you plenty of information to consider and lots of exercises to help you understand it. Take it as slow as you need to, just stick with it. You are worth knowing!

The Cornucopia Method of Manifestation Step II: Know Yourself

A few thousand years ago, seekers of truth came to the Temple of Delphi from all over the ancient world. They sought out the oracle there to answer life's most pressing questions: *Should I marry this person or that one? Will my crops thrive? What should I do for my health? What strategies will prove successful for me in battle? Will I have a child? Who will rule?*

As the pilgrims entered the temple with these issues weighing on their minds, they would have noticed two words carved above the threshold: "Know Thyself." Perhaps the words were meant to alert the seekers that the trip to the temple was not the end of their journey, but only the beginning. For more often than not, the answers offered by the oracle were cryptic, designed to encourage the seeker to engage in intensive self-reflection.

Today, I, too, consult oracular tools such as Tarot. I also teach others how to use them. I would argue that even in modern times, an oracle is only as useful as the querent's level of psycho-spiritual development. Additionally, a divinatory reading does not have a fixed meaning. Instead, the meaning is whatever messages are meaningful to the seeker. I'm not suggesting that the practice of divination lacks value. Instead, I'm proposing that life itself is an enormous Temple of Delphi and that your experiences of reality are oracular, insightful proclamations for you. Unless you know yourself well, however, the messages will be lost on you.

Your Beliefs Shape Your Reality

At this point you may be wondering, "What in the world is she talking about? What does the Oracle at Delphi have to do with me learning to consciously manifest?"

Everything you need to know about how to create the life you want is written in the message of your life. You call this message "reality." Reality is nothing more than a storyline fed back to you by that great cosmic mirror, the Ground Consciousness, in response to the vibrational frequencies your system has emitted. And these frequencies you emit are all based on your Constitutional Belief System.
A belief is a collection of thoughts that the personality has identified as Truth.

Your Constitutional Belief System is the complete package of all the different beliefs operating within your system right now. It was created by the interplay of your unconscious, pre-conscious and conscious thoughts, emotions, physiological sensations, assumptions and experiences. Together these forces create a kind of filter that affects what you perceive. They shape your reality by determining what information you allow in and how you interpret it.

Your brain can only process an infinitesimal amount of the input available in the sights, sounds, sensations and experiences of your environment. To sift through the vast amount of data efficiently and seek out the most relevant information, your mind integrates only what supports your current Constitutional Belief System. Anything else is either disregarded or explained away as an aberration. Moreover, your mind will work (usually outside of your awareness) to bring about events consistent with your Constitutional Belief System.

The process happens like this:

1. Brain receives input.
2. Constitutional Belief System filters out extraneous information (that is, anything inconsistent with the Constitutional Belief System).
3. Individual interprets the remaining information according to Constitutional Belief System, and

4. Individual exhibits behavior consistent with this interpretation.
5. Behavior elicits responses from environment that appear to reinforce Constitutional Belief System.

The ability and tendency of the mind to unconsciously manipulate the environment to support what one expects or believes to be true is supported by a large body of empirical evidence. The "teacher expectancy effect" or "Pygmalion effect," for instance, refers to students' tendencies to better their performance in response to a teacher's expectations. Specifically, if a teacher was told (and therefore believed) that a new student was particularly bright, the teacher would be more responsive to that student. The student's performance then improved. So the teacher's belief prompted certain behavior, and that behavior elicited responses supporting the belief.

Similarly, the "observer effect" or "experimenter effect" refers to a researcher's unconscious influence on variables in a study to support a hypothesis. This is the reason behind good experimental studies where, for instance, neither the research doctors nor participants in a study know which people are receiving a medicine and which are taking a placebo. It's been proven that a researcher's bias can change the results of an experiment.

The same phenomenon occurs in your everyday life. You've probably thought about it as the concept of self-fulfilling prophesy.

Quantum physics explains the self-fulfilling prophesy in this way: nothing exists until it is measured. In other words, there is no real world existing independently of our observation of it, just a lot of probabilities. We bring our reality into being via our observation. And *what we create with our observation depends upon where we bring our awareness.* So your personal reality arises in response to where and how you direct your attention. Similarly, our species creates our collective reality via our collective beliefs and expectations.

Twentieth-century physicist Neils Bohr declared, "If quantum mechanics hasn't profoundly shocked you, you haven't understood it yet." But in some ways, the scientific observations of the last 100 years are nothing new. Science is simply confirming what shamans and mystics have been saying for thousands of years: the experience of material reality is an illusion, and we shape that illusion out of our thoughts and beliefs.

So the reason you notice certain repeating patterns in your business, your relationships and your life is because your belief systems continue to produce the same thoughts. You will get what you (consciously or unconsciously) expect based on your assumptions.

There is a major problem with this setup, and it's this: many people never take the opportunity to question their assumptions. Each of us absorbs familial, cultural, religious and educational assumptions about reality before we can even speak. Some of those assumptions ride in on our DNA. Because we are exposed to these ideas at such a young age, we accept them as Truth. When we mature, most of us will naturally tend to gravitate toward social systems and institutions that feel familiar. As long as things are going smoothly, there's no need to consciously sift through our beliefs to determine what makes sense and what's a little off, what serves us and what's holding us back, what we'd rather let go and what we'd like to keep. So the unevaluated beliefs remain, running our lives for as long as we let them. How can you use this information to improve your success in life, love or business?

You can begin to explore your own Constitutional Belief System to root out Unconscious Limiting Beliefs that keep you from enjoying the life you want to create.

An Unconscious Limiting Belief (ULB) is a belief that operates below conscious awareness to keep you from growing. Every one of your beliefs, including your ULBs, made sense at some point in your life in the context of a particular situation. You adopted them because they worked, or at least made sense based on the information available to you at the time. But if some of your unconscious beliefs are now out of alignment with your conscious goals, you won't realize your dreams, no matter how hard you try. For instance, you have an internal money "set point," similar to the metabolic or weight set point you might hear discussed in health literature. If your internal money set point is lower than your conscious financial goals, something in your life will sabotage you anytime you begin to exceed your unconscious limits. Let's say you want to generate a particular dollar amount in net profit per month in your business. You have a great product and a fantastic team in place. Your market data indicates that you should reach this number easily.

But sales don't measure up to expectations. Or, each time you meet your sales goals, some unexpected expense arises and eats into your profits. When you notice this sort of pattern, you can be sure that your unconscious beliefs do not support your conscious goals.

Here's the good news: life continually provides you with experiences that have the potential to expose your limiting beliefs. (Perhaps you can think of such an experience right now.) These experiences are wake-up calls. They are invitations to examine your assumptions and know yourself more fully. They are openings to your true nature…if you recognize them and decide to walk through with your eyes wide open.

My Wake-Up Calls

When I was eighteen years old, I had a nightmare.

I was driving a car on the highway, watching lightning slice through a menacing black sky. An otherworldly storm was brewing. The wind was blowing so hard I could hardly keep my car on the road. A tractor-trailer began to pass my car in the right lane. As it went by I noticed that it was especially long. The trailers behind the cab turned into enormous orange and white construction barrels. The line of barrels began to jerk erratically and they forced my car off the highway, and I crashed. I climbed out of the car and looked around. Suddenly, everything was quiet. I realized that it was the end of the world and the fate of my soul would be decided at any moment. I began to run and hide, afraid that I would be damned.

I bolted upright in bed, sweating and terrified. Suddenly staying the way I was seemed like the worst fate in the world. I wasn't even sure what was so terrible about life as I knew it. I just knew that it wasn't enough. There was so much to learn and do and be. I wasn't ready to be judged on the basis of who I was in that moment. I said the most earnest prayer of my young life: "God, please help me change. I don't care what it takes. Help me figure out who I'm supposed to be. Help me grow."

I had no clue what I was really asking for, but my prayer was answered beautifully with a series of ego-shattering experiences. For each crisis of meaning and belief, I was fortunate to find resources that helped me create meaning out of the pain. Even so, I still spent many years engaged in a dance of resistance. I wanted to figure out the answer so that I wouldn't have to hurt any more. I wanted to have it all together. For the next decade, as I went to college and graduate school, got married and began my career, I worked hard to control whatever I could control.

Then our first daughter, Maddie, came along — to teach me just how illusory control is.

Maddie was a wild child: sensitive, insightful, brilliant, serious, intense, boundary-pushing. She threw tantrums I swore would tear the house down (or at least provoke a neighbor to call the Division of Family Services). An hour later, tantrum forgotten, she'd be asking me, "Mommy, does the Holy Spirit wear shoes?" or announcing, "Indigo is the color of silence." Mothering Maddie stretched me and tested me and nearly swallowed me up.

One night after a particularly frustrating battle of wills, I locked myself in my sacred-space room, afraid I would hurt my child if I had to stay in her presence one second longer. I lay on the futon in the dark, tears dripping down my face, listening to Maddie scream. I felt like a complete failure. Why was I even considering having another child? I was hopeless with just one. My "having it all together" façade was gone. I wasn't sure I could bear to look at the emptiness underneath.

I picked up the phone to call my mom for some sympathy, but something stopped me, told me to just sit in the silence. Be with the pain. I don't know how long I lay there before I felt a voice inside of me say, "Your failure to be perfect is Maddie's gift to you. Stop trying to figure out how to do it right. Stop trying to figure out how to make her be the way you want her to be. She's here to help you accept yourself the way you are. You don't have to be the perfect mother. You don't have to do it like anyone else has done it before. You only have to be the best mother you can be for her."

Limiting Beliefs Exposed: That I had to be a perfect mother. That Maddie's behavior was a reflection on me. That if she acted out, or tested me, or was unhappy, it meant I was doing something wrong.

Recognizing these limiting beliefs was a huge turning point in my relationship with Maddie and in my life. Now Maddie is a brilliant, beautiful, creative young woman and I feel blessed to be her mother. And the tearing down of my ego, that had to happen for me to be a better mother to her, prepared me for another big challenge: mothering our second child, Bridget.

When Bridget was a few months old, David and I realized she was not developing at a typical rate. Shortly afterward we found out she had a congenital heart defect. The day we went to her cardiologist's office for the first time, I looked at our tiny five-month-old daughter lying on the examination table. Bridget looked back at me. The intensity of her gaze pulled me in. It had all the wisdom and depth of a person many decades older. Suddenly she "spoke" to me. Her voice was actually in my mind, but I heard it as clearly as if she had said the words out loud. "Don't feel sorry for me," she said. "I am not a victim. I chose this life. I came here in this body, to have these experiences. I knew what I was doing. I did it for you. I did it to help you grow. Don't miss it. Don't waste this."

Limiting Beliefs Exposed: That Bridget should have been born healthy. That she should have developed normally. That her heart defect and developmental delays meant that I had done something wrong, or that we were being punished.

The insight Bridget shared with me sustained me over the next few years. Our devastation over the heart defect was only the beginning. For awhile, it seemed like every month she had an appointment with a new specialist. Each doctor would highlight more issues and present opinions about what she'd never be able to do. And then the surgery to correct her defect led to a second open-heart surgery. And then another.

That period of my life is mostly a blur. I did a lot of crying, praying, journaling and reflecting. I wrote poetry. This poem speaks to my process of finally beginning to release resistance:

Unraveling

*Take the knife
that would slice your heart open
and use it to sever
what no longer serves your Destiny.*

*Don't let the wall of your security
crush you as it falls apart.
Dismantle it carefully, stone
by stone and be amazed
at what it kept you from seeing.*

*Open your arms
to the storm*

and let the lightning ignite your soul
and burn away
the rotten remnants
of the false self
you've been wearing.

Let the waves of emotion
knock you from your feet
and tear away the oxygen mask
that always left you wondering
when you would run out of air.

Grab the knife.
Destroy the wall.
Embrace the storm.
Dive into the water.

Stop struggling.
You will not drown.
You will not drown.
You will only learn a new way
to breathe.

EXERCISE: Your Wake-Up Calls

Your life story is, of course, different from mine. And so are your wake-up calls.

What have been your most important, humbling, ego-erasing experiences? What life events caused you to question everything you believed to be true? Are you in the middle of one right now?

If we live long enough, all of us have stories of facing death, loss, trauma and other experiences that shake our foundations.

Take a few minutes to write about some of your transformational experiences and what they taught you about yourself. Are there any unexamined, painful experiences that might still hold learning opportunities for you? Can you revisit them now with a more neutral eye, mining the content without engaging the emotional intensity?

Write about one of those experiences in your journal. Describe the experience briefly and then identify at least one belief that was challenged by what happened. How did you resolve the challenge to your belief(s)? Looking back now, do you have any new insights? (There's no need to stop with one experience if you feel called to write about more.)

Growing Without Suffering

Thanks to my children I finally began to learn, the hard way, that I was creating my own suffering: first, by running away from pain, and later, by relying on painful experiences alone to facilitate my growth.

I'm not implying that life can or should be painfree. Pain is part of life on the material plane. It's part of the full range of experiences you'll have while in a body. There is no way of avoiding it. And when pain comes, you may as well at least get something out if it. You can use the painful situation as a tool to expose limiting beliefs and release ego attachments. So at least pain has some value.

Suffering, however, is neither necessary nor useful. Suffering is the additional pain you create for yourself when you resist your experiences. It happens when you refuse responsibility for the life you've created and insist that things should be somehow other than they are.

Challenging life experiences offer opportunities to let go of limiting beliefs. When you refuse those opportunities, you suffer.

After Bridget was born I realized one of my Unconscious Limiting Beliefs was: if I do everything right during my pregnancy (eat the right foods, avoid toxic substances, exercise, meditate, get energy work, etc.) then my child will be born healthy. If she's not healthy, then it means I did something wrong. After her diagnoses, I had some choices to make about what story I wanted to live with. Choosing to let go of my beliefs around Bridget's health did not free me of pain. But it did save me from a lot of suffering.

Suffering also happens when you claim pain as a badge, or an identity. Can you think of anyone who identifies themselves as a victim of a painful past? Even identifying as a survivor, while perhaps temporarily empowering, traps the survivor in the mindset of a person who has undergone trauma. The victim/survivor identity constantly focuses the person's awareness on the difficulties of the past, thereby tainting the experience of the present and expectations of the future.

Religion sometimes feeds into a martyr/victim identification by presenting images of holy suffering as a path to salvation. I agree that pain can be instructive and even necessary to growth. But suffering for suffering's sake, in my mind, is just another form of ego aggrandizement: a way for the personality to prove its worth or specialness when there is really nothing to prove. It's much easier, and less painful, just to remember who you really are. (You are Essence, in case you need a reminder).

I've tried many different forms of suffering in my life and I expect you have, too. I can't recommend any of them. I'd like to help you avoid more suffering if I can.

While I won't pretend I can guarantee you a life free from suffering, I do believe that if you follow the concepts in this course and practice your Manifestation Matrix Meditation, growth will become an even more natural experience. It will become more conscious. You won't need to rely on painful wake-up calls like shock, stress, accidents or illness to catapult you into consciousness. And when pain does arrive, you will feel it. You will be able to be present to its message. You will honor it, without identifying with it. And eventually, I hope, you will be able to go beyond the pain and see that situation as the gift that it is. In short, life will get easier for you.

So let's explore some short cuts to exposing your limiting beliefs without suffering.

Recognizing Unconscious Limiting Beliefs

Limiting beliefs are ideas that made sense for you at one time, but are now holding you back from experiencing and expressing the fullness of Who You Are. Many limiting beliefs are acquired in childhood and are necessarily limiting when applied in your adult life. But typically, such beliefs are unconscious. So, the obvious question arises: what are you supposed to do about a limiting belief if you aren't even aware that you have it? How can you know when an Unconscious Limiting Belief is operating in your life?

Your emotions are your best barometer. Often feelings of anxiety, anger, frustration, cynicism and the like are indications that your unconscious beliefs about what you can have, be or do are not in alignment with your Authentic Desires.

Conscious Manifestation Secret

Whenever you are experiencing an uncomfortable emotion or physical sensation, that's your cue to get very alert. Ask yourself: *Can I identify any thoughts or storylines that go along with these uncomfortable emotions or feelings?* If so, where do those thoughts lead? What are the underlying assumptions involved here that you haven't examined before? What might you have swallowed as truth that could be questioned at this juncture?

The process of examining old beliefs can be unwieldy if you're going at it on your own, so I'd like to make it easier for you by listing some of the limiting beliefs you'll probably encounter in yourself. Unconscious Limiting Beliefs are as varied and unique as the people who have them. However, I've noticed nine beliefs common to Western culture that get in the way of success and happiness. Most of the other beliefs I've encountered are related to these nine:

The Nine Most Common
Unconscious Limiting Beliefs:

1. Money creates happiness/unhappiness.
2. There's only so much to go around.
3. My results are determined by outside forces.
4. Nothing good comes easy.
5. My past predicts my future.
6. Service equals sacrifice.
7. It takes money to make money.
8. Timing is everything.
9, My happiness is in the future (I'll be happy when _____)

As we explore each of the nine most common Unconscious Limiting Beliefs, you will have the opportunity to consider where they might be operating in your own life. Later we will look at what you can do to transform those Unconscious Limiting Beliefs into Conscious Empowering Experiences.

Unconscious Limiting Belief (ULB) #1
Money Creates Happiness/Unhappiness

The first common Unconscious Limiting Belief (ULB) is that money makes you happy, or, alternatively, that money makes you miserable. Let's begin with the idea that money creates happiness. Perhaps you've thought to yourself that if you could only have a certain income per month, your problems would be solved.

I'm not bashing money. I love to play with money. I enjoy having it. I like to generate it, spend it, save it, give it away, think about it and wonder at it. However, the idea that money creates happiness is actually backwards. What is true is that *happiness creates wealth*. Why is that? Well, when you encounter people who are positive and happy, don't you like to be around them? Aren't they fun? Those kinds of people attract other people, and they attract opportunity.

Happiness brings about true wealth in all of its forms. The etymology of the word "wealth" is well-being. True wealth, therefore, incorporates money, health, relationships, time to do the things you want to do and having meaning and purpose in your day-to-day existence. When you remember to *fall in love* with life, wealth is the low-hanging fruit on a lush and verdant tree.

When was the last time you got into the shower and turned on the water and were happy that water came out of that faucet? Do you ever get excited about the fact that you can flip a switch and produce light? Have you ever lain on the ground under a spectacular sky and watched the stars spinning around you for so long that you became grateful to the earth for holding you close to her and keeping you from getting lost in space? Do you watch your children sleeping and wonder that you could ever love that much? Have you ever woken up to a sound that you later recognized as your own breathing and given thanks for the awareness that you are alive for another day? Have you ever caught an unexpected sight of your beloved and forgotten, just for a moment, who he or she was, and then felt happy all over as you realized this person was in love with you and was your partner in life? Do you ever catch yourself smiling for no reason? Try it. When you show up for life in this way, you will be amazed at what happens.

The belief that money makes you unhappy is just as common as the belief that it makes you happy. I'm sure you can think of numerous examples of people who had tons of money and miserable lives. The problem is equating the money with the misery. Money doesn't make people happy or unhappy. What it can do is highlight our personalities because it allows us to inject those personalities more powerfully in the material world. It's likely we both know people who use money as a tool to exercise inappropriate power over other people. But I don't believe for a second that it's the money that gives those people the craving for power.

EXERCISE:

Think about what sort of negative messages, expressed or implied, you picked up at home, school and religious institutions about money. Here are a few common examples: *Money is the root of all evil. Rich people are mean. Rich people got their money by oppressing others. It's easier for a camel to go through the eye of the needle than it is for a rich man to go to heaven.* (The eye of the needle, by the way, is a biblical reference to a particular mountain pass in the Middle East, NOT a sewing needle).

How have those negative ideas about money impacted your ability to create the lifestyle you want, or to enjoy the money you have?

Take a few moments to write in your journal in regard to any beliefs about money making you happy or unhappy that you inherited from your family, school, culture, friends and religion. You might be surprised to find that you've been carrying contradictory beliefs: money makes you happy AND money makes you miserable! How might your conflicting, polarizing or otherwise limiting beliefs be impacting the way you relate to money?

ULB #2: There's Only So Much to Go Around (also known as Scarcity or Limited Supply)

The next common Unconscious Limiting Belief is that your access to energy, time, money, love, food or whatever resources you need is limited. The belief in limited supply is so deeply rooted that it is the foundation of our economy (supply and demand). Limited supply is the source of all other limiting beliefs.

Because appearances are so persuasive, you might be tempted to argue that limited supply is *not* an Unconscious Limiting Belief at all, but an accurate assessment of how things operate in the material world. I'm sure you've had experiences that demonstrated the reality of scarcity to you. When you were a child, your parents divided their attention between you and other people. You were told to share your toys. You may have been instructed to finish the food on your plate because other people, somewhere in the world, were starving.

As you've grown older, you've continued to have experiences that reinforced the appearance of limitation. You've lost people you loved. You've run out of time to do the things you wanted to do. You've learned to budget your money (or at least maybe felt like you should learn how to do that, someday). You've experienced gasoline prices going up in response to warnings that the earth was running out of oil. You've seen droughts, witnessed famines and watched our species wage war after war over access to territory and natural resources.

But as painful as these conflicts and losses have been, they've all sprung from our species' collective belief in separation and scarcity. If we could remember our connection to Essence, if we were taught from childhood how to access that Cornucopia of abundance, then we'd have all the energy in the universe at our fingertips. And we could use it to produce whatever we needed.

The illusion of scarcity persists because of ego attachments to form. Once you release those attachments, you realize there is always plenty of everything you need. There is always more love, although that love may have a different face than the one you're used to seeing. There is always more money. The illusion of the dwindling bank account and the looming debt is simply a game to help you learn how to attract the prosperity you desire. There is always more energy. And perhaps humanity will need to call upon its collective creative power to figure out how to tap energy in ways that will fuel our desires.

How do you know if the Unconscious Limiting Belief of scarcity is operating in your life? It's there whenever you act out of a fear of running out. Or a fear that someone else might get what you want — or take away something you have. The belief in scarcity is underneath every worry. It keeps you from risking what you've got, even if you aren't that happy with it, to go after what you really want (a bird in the hand is worth two in the bush).

The belief in limited supply or scarcity also gives rise to guilt and steals your enjoyment of what you have. It makes you feel that whatever you have comes at the expense of someone else.

Melinda was a client whose Unconscious Limiting Belief in scarcity kept her from enjoying her success. Melinda owned a small business that employed over twenty people. Her intelligence, business savvy, management skills and focused, creative energy helped Melinda develop a lucrative income from her company. She consciously groomed an effective team that could run day-to-day operations whenever she was out of the office. But every time she took a day off or worked from home she felt guilty because her employees had to be at work. And if she went on vacation to a beautiful spot, her enjoyment was typically marred by feelings of guilt that her employees were working while she was on vacation, or that they would not be able to afford a trip like the one she had taken.

As Melinda worked with the Cornucopia concepts, she began to understand that enjoying what she had created for herself did not take something away from her employees. Conversely, limiting her pleasure did not benefit her employees or anyone else who had less than she did. She began to enjoy her work more as she became increasingly comfortable in her role as an employer. Melinda realized she was giving something of value to her employees: a great place to work. She understood that every person who worked for her had his or her own ability to connect with

Essence, and that they could use that energy to create what they most desired. Interestingly, as Melinda worked with The Manifestation Matrix Meditation, she found that her employees also seemed to enjoy *their* work more. Those few whose attitudes had been negatively affecting others in the office began leaving the company. They were replaced with people who were enthusiastic and committed to their work. Everyone in the company benefited from Melinda's decision to release her Unconscious Limiting Belief in scarcity.

Your separation from Essence, the Source of all creation, is an illusion. Believe the illusion and it appears that supply is limited. But look behind the veil and you'll realize that all you need to do is "ask and it is given." The universe has been expanding ever since the Big Bang. Your consciousness is part of that expansion.

One of my meditation practices is to silently repeat a sacred passage. This is a poem I dwell on each day:

Everything you see
has its roots in the unseen world.
The forms may change but the essence
remains the same.

Every wondrous sight will vanish
every sweet word shall fade.
But do not be disheartened.
The Source they come from
is eternal, growing, branching out
bringing new life
and new joy.

Why do you weep?
That Source is within you
and this whole world
is springing up from it.

The Source is full
its waters are ever flowing.
Do not grieve; drink your fill.
Don't think it will ever run out.
This is the endless ocean.

-Jalaluddin Rumi, Sufi Poet and Mystic

When you remember your access to the Unified Field, you know about the inexhaustible Cornucopia. You know there's always more. More of everything. More money, more resources, more energy, more ideas. There are no limits.

EXERCISE:
Where in your life have you bought into the idea of limited supply? Have you held yourself back from what you really want because you were afraid that it would deprive someone else? Or convinced yourself that you've already received your fair share of money, love, happiness, beauty, excitement, experiences?

Conversely, where in your life have you experienced jealousy? Jealousy comes from an unconscious belief in scarcity — the idea that if someone else has what you want, it's not available for you. Have you ever made up a story that if someone was wealthy, or famous or happy in a relationship, those experiences came at the expense of someone or something else? How do you know if that's true? And even if it is true, have you ever wondered whether there might also be examples of people who got ahead by helping others, by serving the planet? **Write your reflections in your journal.**

ULB #3: My Results Are Determined by Outside Forces

The next Unconscious Limiting Belief is that your success or failure is determined by something outside of yourself: the economy, other people, circumstances, family history, ethnicity, gender…you name it. People offer all sorts of reasons for not having the lives they claim to want. Business coach Dan Kennedy says that you can have excuses or you can have success, but you can't have both.

He's right. You create your own reality, your own economy and your own success (or failure). And if you've really created your own reality, then you created whatever situation you were born into, along with everything that came after that.

A lot of people don't like this idea. When you are disappointed by what is happening in your life, it might seem easier to think of yourself as a victim of fate. Perhaps accepting responsibility for your results will feel easier *if you re-define failure.*

I used to be a consummate perfectionist. I worked very hard to prove myself but no matter how well I did it was never enough to free me from the fear of failing. In high school I went to the state oratory finals two years in a row. Instead of celebrating these achievements, I was devastated because I didn't win. When I was in college I had anxiety attacks whenever I thought I might ruin my 4.0 GPA with a B grade. Romantic relationships were painful because every one that didn't work out (defined at that point in my life as ending in marriage) was evidence of my inherent flaws.

I believed that in order to have love and security, I had to do everything exceptionally well. I had to be everything to everyone. I did my best to present an image of having it all together, all the time. Each perceived failure threatened to expose me as a fraud.

Of course, I wasn't fooling anyone with this perfection façade. I only made myself miserable. Fortunately, I eventually adopted some new ideas about success and failure.

Once I took responsibility for my life I began to see that every result that turned out differently than what my ego wanted was a gift. I couldn't always see the gift, but I learned to trust that at the very least there was something I could learn from in every experience.

Every experience is a learning opportunity. And whether I've lost money or something else, viewing the experience through the lens of what I've learned takes the sting out of it for me. When loss is learning, then I don't need to look for something or someone to blame. I don't need to make up a story about why this experience happened to me. I can trust that I created it for my own benefit.

So take failure out of your vocabulary. And take responsibility for all of your results.

EXERCISE:

Think of a time you felt like a failure, a time you did not achieve the results you were hoping for. What stories did you tell yourself about that experience? What did you learn from the experience? How can you apply that learning in your life right now? **Write your insights in your journal.**

ULB #4: Nothing Good Comes Easy

The next Unconscious Limiting Belief is that achieving your dreams must be difficult because nothing good comes easy (no pain, no gain).

The idea that happiness is a reward for working hard would be fine—if by hard work you meant the natural satisfaction that arises when you put your whole self into whatever you are doing. When you are fully present, when you know you are giving your best and enjoying the creative process, your work is a reward in itself. But that's not what most people mean when they say "no pain no gain." They really mean that happiness is a reward for suffering.

Do *you* know anyone whose self-inflicted suffering has actually led to happiness?

When I worked as an associate for a law firm, I was surrounded by unhappy people. Morale fell to such a low point, the partners took everyone on a retreat to try toimprove the situation. At the retreat our discussion quickly disintegrated into a litany of complaints. We young associates were an unhappy bunch. One of the partners, we'll call him George, stood up and started yelling at the people who had expressed dissatisfaction. He was shaking as he said, "Who told you work would make you happy? You work hard and then if you're lucky someday you'll enjoy the fruits of your labors. Quit griping and just do your jobs. You're not supposed to be having fun."

Wow.

None of the other partners disputed his opinion, so I assumed they agreed with it. I think he's still there, presumably feeling smug about how hard he's working and looking forward to the day he might get to be happy.

As for me, I got the hell out of there.

I haven't regretted it once. I'm finding that as long as I regularly connect with Essence, *many good things DO come easily*.

Go with the flow. It's a lot more fun than doing something you don't enjoy in hopes that someday fate will reward your sacrifice.

EXERCISE:

Strategic planning and short-term sacrifices can be marvelous choices if they serve a larger, life-purpose level goal (and, of course, if they create a feeling of joyful expectancy in you because of that larger purpose). When you are directing your energy to service your dreams, it's easier to say no to distractions. But many people confuse this sort of conscious choice making with continuing to labor on at something long after they've forgotten why they decided to do it.

Are there any areas in your life that aren't working, but you've kept pushing ahead with them in hopes of a future reward? What sacrifices are you making? (And what could you be doing instead?) What do you hope to gain? And is the reward you are working toward worth the sacrifices to your current happiness? **Write your reflections in your journal.**

ULB #5: The Past Predicts the Future

The next Unconscious Limiting Belief is that your past predicts your future. This belief is only as accurate as you let it be. Many people do repeat unhappy patterns from their pasts, but only because they are unconsciously re-creating the same situations, looking for a different and more satisfying resolution. You don't need to do that. Each moment holds the possibility of creating something new and fresh.

When I was a psychotherapist, I saw people recover from what you might imagine to be irrevocably crippling pasts. I watched people heal wounds that had been wreaking havoc in their families for generations.

The past is nothing more than a collection of stories your mind has created about your experiences. In fact, you can change who you are in the present by *re-imagining* your past. Your body, which is emitting the vibrations that create your reality, knows no difference between a current story you make up about what happened and what actually happened. And if you play with this concept enough, you will see that the idea of a particular past that *really* happened is actually pretty flimsy.

But many people waste a lot of energy, making up limiting stories about today, based on whatever limiting stories they made up about yesterday.

Michel was a real estate investor. His experience in business had been "you can't trust anyone." He was afraid to disclose information about potential projects when he was establishing new business relationships because he expected people to steal his ideas and his deals. He'd "been burned too many times." He often said things like, "This is a dog-eat-dog business," and "That deal's a disaster waiting to happen."

Not surprisingly, Michel often proved himself right. His taciturn, suspicious nature did not create an atmosphere for fun, easy deals. He did sometimes make good money on his investments, but perhaps not as much as he would have had he cultivated more amicable business relationships. And he probably missed out on some opportunities altogether due to his negative attitude. He certainly had been through some challenging experiences in his business, but those experiences were now consuming him. He was allowing them to color and *limit* everything he did.

When Michel first came to see me, he was not enjoying his work. But he was convinced that any other business would be just as bad because he'd "still have to deal with people." I encouraged Michel to start noticing the way he talked about his business. He was skeptical that his words had any affect on the outcomes of his deals (he said he talked about life this way because it was true!), but he was willing to experiment and see what happened. Many of our sessions consisted of me interrupting him every few sentences and challenging him to consider whether his statements were always true. Could he think of ANY examples where a deal had gone off without a hitch? Or where a person on the other side of a deal proved to be trustworthy?

After a few sessions Michel became pretty adept at catching his own limiting language. He created new statements about his present experiences based on a more expansive picture of his past. He ended up deciding to stay in real estate because he was enjoying it more.

The only reality that is important is now. If the now you are experiencing is not making you happy, understand, with compassion and forgiveness, that you created it out of your past consciousness, thoughts, words, emotions, feelings, actions and results. The fastest path to experiencing a new reality is to bring the full power of your presence to what is happening right here, right now.

When you find yourself caught in an old pattern, take a deep breath. Silently repeat a mantram (a holy word or phrase you've chosen as a mind-focusing tool—you'll find more discussion of the mantram in the section on Step V: Be Here Now). Notice your thoughts. Notice your feelings and emotions. Take another breath. Now bring your awareness back to the moment you're experiencing. By engaging your whole self, you have the creative capacity to respond to your current reality in a fresh way. And that automatically catapults you out of the rut you've been in. So no matter what is happening in your life right now, show up for it. Be fully present. You will be amazed at how quickly new possibilities will begin to emerge for you.

Terrible Beauty

A sky like that
ought to be enough
even for the most intransigent
heart.

Just look at it:
light-laden coral clouds
cascading across a cornflower
canvas, coaxing me to thaw
my frozen feelings
in the face of their phenomenal
fire.

And yet, I stand
unmoved.

What use have I
for heartbreaking beauty?
I'm holding a heart already
a hundred times broken.

So surround me with sunsets,
beleaguer me with beauty.
Tonight the only tender
thing that I can do
is make space for one
who cannot even weep for
wonder.

EXERCISE:
List in your journal some of the statements you make
about yourself that include the words "always," "never"
and "all." Those words are often indications that your mind
is writing a current script based on an old story. For
instance, you might think, *Those things never work out for me,*
or *I'm always running late* or *All of my bosses have been jerks; if I*
leave this job I'll just end up with another jerk boss anyway.
"Always," "never" and "all" are rarely accurate.

Another one to watch for is *I'm no good at...* Of course, as
long as you continue to say that, it will be true.

Take a close look at the stories you continue to create for
yourself out of your past experiences. Notice when you hear
yourself telling stories about what people have done to you,
how you have suffered, how your luck is bad. Start making
up new statements that reflect where you want to be.
Change the way you language your present reality. Take
baby steps. Choose words that make you feel a little bit
better about your situation. Find examples from your own
life or someone else's life that support your new words.

The key is to make it believable for you. If Michel, the
businessman from a few pages ago, would have jumped

right from "disaster waiting to happen" to "all of my business associates have my best interests at heart," some part of his unconscious would have balked. He wouldn't have been able to take it in because it was at such odds with where he had been. But by instead saying things such as "I know that some people are honest. I am moving in the direction of working with people I can trust," that seemed believable to him. And once he had lived in that vibration for a little while, he could nudge himself a little more.

Identify one language pattern you recognize in yourself that ties you to a past pattern you'd like to break. Write down the words you've tended to use and then write something that feels a little bit better. Read the new words out loud and then notice where they register in your body. Keep nudging your words in the direction of the experience you would like to be having. Stay with the process for as long as it feels productive.

ULB #6: Service Equals Sacrifice

The next Unconscious Limiting Belief is that service equals sacrifice. This belief is easy to recognize because it typically shows up in martyr-like behavior. You can trace it back to the idea of limited supply: if I am going to help you then I have to sacrifice myself because we can't BOTH be happy. If your slice of the pie gets bigger, then mine must get smaller. The funny thing about the "service equals sacrifice" model is that usually the people who are living out this belief (and I used to be one of them) are no fun to be around. They spend most of their energy letting you know how hard they've worked for you and saying things like "Can't you see how much I love you? I did this and that for you and it was so difficult..." (insert heavy sigh here). Of course, few people enjoy hanging out with a martyr. Service is a lovely idea, however.

The best sort of service you can give another person or the planet is to figure out what your unique gifts are and then express them. When you are doing what you are really good at and what you enjoy, everybody wins. Martyrdom is just no fun!

EXERCISE:

In his powerful and planet-transforming book, *A New Earth*, Eckhart Tolle suggests in each moment to bring your awareness to one of three attitudes: enthusiasm, enjoyment or acceptance. Even if you can't bring yourself to enjoy cleaning the litter box, for instance, or waking up in the night to feed your child, you can certainly shift your attitude to acceptance: (*This is a task I'm choosing to do in this moment because it needs to be done. It will be more satisfying for me to complete this than to leave it undone*). I would contend that you can often flip from acceptance right into gratitude, even in the midst of a hated chore. (*I'm so glad I have this cat. She is a great friend to me. She always greets me when I come home. It feels good when she sits on my lap and purrs.*)

Tolle contends that if you can't bring yourself into a place of acceptance around an activity, you need to stop doing it, at least until you can conjure an accepting attitude. I agree. I remember the times I had to lay my colicky, screaming babies in their cribs after they had cried for hours because I just couldn't do it anymore. I wished I could be more present to their needs, but in that moment, I couldn't. I was concerned that my deteriorating state of mind would be more harmful to them than taking a few minutes to pull myself back together. I returned when I could manage an attitude of acceptance.

What about you? Are there any tasks that regularly give rise to resentment in you? Is it possible to shift your attitude around those activities? And, if not, what might that indicate about changes you could make in your life?

Consider the role you are playing during the troublesome activity: parent, spouse, child, friend, caregiver, employer, employee. Then write out this sentence: "A good _____ " (fill in the blank with your particular role) and then make a list. For instance, "a good mom is always available for her children." Now make a list for the same role in the negative: "A good _____ does not _____" i.e., "a good mom never allows her infant to cry." Identify at least 5-10 words or phrases for each list. Now, take a look at the list. Where do those rules come from? Whose rules are they? Whom do they serve? Are they relevant to your life today? Which ones might you like to revise or eliminate and which would you like to keep?

A good _____ (write the list in your journal)

A good _____ does not _____ (write the list in your journal)

Continue this exercise for any roles you'd like to examine. (Hint: take a look at all the tasks or situations where you experience resentment on a regular basis).

ULB #7: It Takes Money to Make Money

The next Unconscious Limiting Belief is that it takes money to make money. I don't believe this was ever true, but it's certainly not true now. Having money can sometimes create a more direct or swift path to more money, but it's not the exclusive path. In fact, most of the wealthiest people in the U.S. right now are first generation millionaires. Often, their lack of money created the deep desire for more that drove them to success.

There are many industries where you can create wealth without any or with only a small initial investment of capital. For instance, information marketing is probably the fastest growing type of business in the world. It's one of the best businesses for making money without having money to invest because you're selling what you already have: information you've gained from your experience. In information marketing, you sell ideas and information that people are happy to pay for because it will improve their lives, save them time or help them to get a job done correctly. Sometimes you can sell ideas and information without producing a physical product at all because the information can be delivered via teleconference lines or digital download.

But even more traditional businesses, such as real estate, offer opportunities for wealth creation with investments of time, energy and ideas rather than money. In many industries, even if your business idea does require capital, you can use other people's money. Using other people's money to make money is a win-win because someone with wealth in the form of money can partner with someone whose wealth is held in time and talent. Each offers a valuable contribution and both benefit.

The most important investment you need to make if you do want to have more money is the investment in yourself. That may come in the form of money you spend to get training or information that will benefit your life. Or traveling somewhere to spend time with a person who can teach and inspire you. Most of the discretionary money I spend goes into expanding my knowledge and my consciousness, because I know I am the most important factor in the success of my business. If I am not growing and expanding, then my business isn't either.

It is also worth noting that often you can manifest what you want without earning money, or spending any money at all. I've experienced material manifestations of countless things I've wished for—sometimes on the very same day! Just a few examples: a gift basket full of bread from a particular local bakery whose products I'd been craving that morning; a scrying mirror, just when I'd decided I wanted to learn how to scry (and I had not shared that desire with anyone); a computer program; show tickets; and a cruise for my family.

When Maddie was a baby I decided I wanted to cut my work schedule to part-time so I could be home with her. The problem was, we were counting on my full-time salary to get by. David and I both felt though, that our family would work better and be happier if I were home more. So, I gave notice to my boss that I wanted to go part-time. A couple of weeks later, David received an unanticipated, unprecedented salary raise that compensated for my reduced income. In that case, not only did we not need money to make money, we suddenly attracted more money when we had less!

EXERCISE:

Are there any dreams you've given up on because you thought it would take too much money to get started? If money were not a factor, what would your wildest dreams call you to create? Let yourself stay in that dream for a while, really imagine what it would be like to live it. **Now write about that dream as if it is happening right now. Include as much detail as possible. Read it out loud.** Notice what is happening in your body. If you have resistance coming up, that's great. Just put your hand on any uncomfortable places in your body. Keep breathing. Notice the thoughts and the storylines. Go back to your dream. Stay with this process, even if it takes coming back to it over a few days. Stay with it until you can experience the positive feelings that come from living that dream, or until your dream shifts to something even more spectacular.

ULB #8: Timing Is Everything

The next Unconscious Limiting Belief is that you need to wait until: everything is perfect; you have a master, long-term plan of action; and you are certain of the outcome before you act on your dreams.

What most people mean when they say they need to wait until the time is right is that they're scared. They are frightened of failure, or of success. They don't know who they'll become if they step into the unknown.

I'm not suggesting that waiting is never appropriate. But be very clear what you are waiting for—and why. If you are waiting for certainty or perfection, then get moving and see what happens.

The universe responds to action. Do something. Anything. And if you want to break out of a rut, just do something different than you'd normally do. The feedback you need to move you closer to your goals will come as a result of your movement.

My husband is a private pilot. He flies for fun. Let's say he wants to go from St. Louis, where we live, to Kansas City. Before he can take off, he's required to file a flight plan. He knows where he's going. But he doesn't wait until he has a perfect plan for getting from here to there without any deviations before he takes off. If he did that, he'd never leave the runway. Flying is an activity that requires constant course correction. As soon as your wheels pull up from the runway, you're off course. You have to constantly factor in the wind, changing weather patterns, other planes. And sometimes you get up there and figure out you have to go somewhere other than where you'd planned. An unexpected storm arises, or your plane has a problem. Once in awhile you might even turn around and go back where you came from and start again another day. But every one of those experiences is feedback that empowers you to make an informed decision about the next course correction.

That's how life is. You don't know for sure ahead of time how the world will respond to what you're putting out there. You can't even be sure that YOU will respond in the way you expect. But if you don't get the response you were expecting–that is fabulous information because then you can be pleasantly surprised or make some changes. Feedback is information that either helps you get closer to your stated goal or get clarity on what you want your new goals to be.

EXERCISE:
What dream have you been putting off until the right time? What's really stopping you? How important is this dream to the quality of your life? **Rate it on a scale of 1-10. If it's at least an 8, set a goal date right now for realizing this dream.** Don't worry about exactly how this will happen, but do set it just far enough out to be accepted by your unconscious as at least possible.

Write your Goal date in your journal.

If you wanted to realize this dream, **what would be the next small step you would need to take RIGHT NOW to begin to bring it into form? Write it down.**

Now, commit to yourself to do that one small thing within the next 48 hours. Write down exactly what you are going to do and the date and time by which it will be complete:

ULB #9: My Happiness is in the Future
(I'll be happy when _____)

The final common Unconscious Limiting Belief we'll be covering is: I'll be happy when _____ happens. I will be happy when my partner treats me better. I will be happy when my child gets through her next heart surgery. I will be happy when my friend realizes that what I want for

112

him is really the best. Your story may be different, but you get the point. You fall into this ULB whenever you decide you can't be happy until something happens.

The truth is that your joy is in this present moment, whatever is happening. Remember the very first ULB we talked about–money creating happiness? No thing, situation or experience creates happiness. Happiness or joy is an existential state that arises out of you and is available to you anytime you bring your full self into the present. The problem with waiting for joy or trying to control events to bring it about is that it tears us away from the only place we can really experience joy: in the now.

Many people scatter their consciousness. They worry about the future. Or ruminate over the past. Only the smallest part of their mind is available to focus and support their goals.

Scientists suggest that most of us are using only 10% of our brains. I believe this is happening, at least in part, because the other 90% is engaged in the past and the future. If you could bring even 50% of your consciousness into the present moment, you would be unstoppable. There wouldn't be anything in the world you couldn't accomplish.

As you become more and more conscious, you will cultivate an increasingly powerful influence over, and insight into, the experiences you call into your life. And regardless of what is happening in your experience, one thing is always in your ultimate control: where you choose to place your awareness. You choose your attitude. You can find something to be grateful for in each moment. You can stop waiting. You can choose to be happy NOW.

Victor Frankl, a prominent figure in Existential Psychotherapy and the author of *Man's Search for Meaning*, developed his theories about the nature of humanity during his experiences as a prisoner in a Nazi concentration camp. Frankl observed that, "Everything can be taken from a [person] but one thing: the last of the human freedoms – to choose one's attitude in any given set of circumstances, to choose one's own way." Frankl found that even in the bleakest of situations, there was power in the choice to be present and to control his own attitude.

Whenever I find myself imagining that I can't find any joy until something happens in the future, I remember Victor Frankl. If he could manage to experience beauty and connection and love and hope while he was in a Nazi death camp instead of deciding (with ample justification, one might argue) that he couldn't be happy until he got out of there...well, surely I can manage to be here now, and find my joy in this moment.

EXERCISE:

Where have you decided to put off happiness until later? How have you been missing out on your life by sending your energy into the future? Think about the times you've said *I can't wait until...* or *if only....*Did the anticipated happiness ever arrive as a result of a hoped for event? And if so, how long did your happiness last?

Choose one area of your life where you've been waiting for something to happen or someone to change. Find at least one thing you can appreciate about that situation RIGHT NOW, even if it's only that you are learning what you don't want. That's no small thing. Appreciate the wisdom that gives you.

Now bring your awareness to something about which you are truly grateful, in any area of your life. Keep your attention there until you can feel that gratitude well up in your body. Let your gratitude create a safe place inside of yourself, a place that is available at any moment. There is always something to appreciate.

Write down what you most appreciate about your life in this moment.

Conscious Empowering Experiences

Congratulations! You've explored all nine of the common Unconscious Limiting Beliefs. Now that you recognize some of your own limiting beliefs, how can you keep them from sabotaging your dreams?

Assuming you've already worked through all of the exercises in this section, another beneficial activity would be to go back through the nine ULBs and see if they trigger an awareness of any other limiting beliefs you've been carrying that you'd now like to release.

Sometimes awareness is all you need to transform a belief that's been holding you back; the light of understanding drains the old belief of its power. But often what you'll notice at first is that you're aware of the belief and how it limits you, but you still can't seem to change your behavior.

You return to habitual behaviors because they are comfortable. They worked well at one time in your life. They worked so well, in fact, that you created strong and deep neural pathways in your brain to support them. When you are in doubt, under stress or unaware, you still move toward the oft-used neural pathways like a wagon wheel that naturally slips into a big rut in a dirt road.

Breaking free from habitual behaviors requires building a repertoire of Conscious Empowering Experiences — new reference points strong enough to overcome the pull toward habitual responses.

How do you come by Conscious Empowering Experiences? I'm glad you asked. By following the next three steps of The Cornucopia Method of Manifestation, of course!

Just to review, the first two steps of The Cornucopia Method of Manifestation are: **I. Set An Intention** and **II. Know Yourself**. You've explored the most challenging two steps already. If you continue practicing setting conscious intentions and being honest with yourself, the next three steps will come more easily to you. The next three steps of The Cornucopia Method of Manifestation are: **III. Befriend Your Body, IV. Raise Your Vibration** and **V. Be Here Now.** To give you a taste of what's in store as you continue to evolve, let's transform those nine common ULBs into Conscious Empowering Experiences.

- "Money creates happiness" becomes: **Happiness creates wealth**

- "There's only so much to go around" becomes: **I am part of an ever-expanding Universe and I have access to every possibility I can imagine**

- "My success or failure is determined by outside forces" becomes: **I create my own economy, my own reality and my own results**

- "Nothing good comes easy" becomes: **As I go with the flow, the Universe constantly surprises me with exciting and enjoyable opportunities**

- "My past predicts my future" becomes: **I create a fresh new reality moment to moment**

- "Service equals sacrifice" becomes: **The highest service I can offer the planet is the discovery and expression of my unique gifts**

- "It takes money to make money" becomes: **Every resource I need to realize my Authentic Desires comes to me as I need it**

- "Timing is everything" becomes: **Inspired action brings me the feedback I need to get me closer to my Authentic Desires**

- "My happiness is in the future" becomes: My joy is in the present moment

EXERCISE:

Review the notes from this section in your journal. Did you identify Unconscious Limiting Beliefs that are unique to you? Rewrite them as Conscious Empowering Experiences. How does it feel to read those empowering words? What happens when you read them out loud? As you continue to work through the five steps of the Cornucopia Method of Manifestation and practice The Manifestation Matrix Meditation, those Conscious Empowering Experiences will become your reality. (Check the resources section on page 188 for the link to download the Manifestation Matrix Meditation audio if you have not already done so).

Now let's move on to Step III: Befriend Your Body.

The Cornucopia Method of Manifestation Step III: Befriend Your Body

Helping people learn how to bring their consciousness into their bodies was one of the most common issues I dealt with as a counselor. Disconnection from the body is so prevalent in our culture that most people don't even recognize it as a problem.

Science now supports what ancient wisdom has known all along: your body lives within a field of energy. Ideally, the field extends approximately an arm's length in all directions, enclosing the body like an egg. There are different names for the energetic field; many people call it the aura, or simply the soul. It is the consciousness that joins with your body to create a living human person. This energy field is what alerts you when someone walks up behind you or otherwise invades your space.

It's likely that you don't live with your consciousness surrounding your body the majority of the time. When I feel into most clients' fields, what I notice is that, instead of encasing the body, the field extends up above the head and only connects with the upper part of the body. Alternatively, the field surrounds the body but it is diffuse, without any clear boundaries. Other times there are voids, energy leaks or dense/stuck energy in the field. All of these are indicators of a mind-body disconnect.

When I was younger I was rarely in my body. As a result I was so accident prone my parents joked that my guardian angels might be killed in the line of duty. My legs are covered with old scars from bicycle crashes and falling down staircases. In my teens and early 20s I had so many car wrecks that my Dad would ask when I called home from college, "Did you crash the car again?" I routinely ran into walls and furniture and twisted my ankles, even as a young adult. It wasn't until I was almost 30 that I associated my clumsiness with a lack of body awareness. Now when I fall or run into things, it is a reminder to get back into my body.

At one time human beings were in tune with their bodies and the earth. A Native American song teaches that the Earth is our Mother. The word "matter" comes from the Latin "mother." And Judeo-Christian scriptures state that human bodies are made from the very clay of the planet. So why are many modern people so cut off from the physical experience?

Somehow, many centuries ago, we began to view our connection with the earth as shameful rather than sacred. We began to believe that our bodies separated us from the god that lived far away in the Temples of the Sky, on the Mountaintops or in the Heavens. We viewed our earth experience as a sentence we must serve for countless lifetimes, or a testing ground to see if we were worthy to live with our God in some other place than this.

That mindset that elevates the mind and denigrates the body is beginning to heal, but the long-term ramifications are still evident in our culture. We are conditioned to live in our heads. At home, school and later the workplace, we are taught to rely only on our brains to guide us. Author Eckhart Tolle argues that most of us have even gone beyond relying on our brains to identifying completely with our thoughts.

Trauma is another factor separating consciousness from the body. All of us have experienced trauma at some point in our lives. Being shamed by people in positions of authority, losing a loved one, witnessing, inflicting or being subjected to violence...all of these experiences cause bits of consciousness to hide or flee the body to survive the trauma. Psychologists call this phenomenon "dissociation;" shamans call it "soul loss." Dissociation or soul loss is a functional short-term coping mechanism. It can even be an initiatory experience, awakening intuition. But if part of your soul has flown off, you'll never be whole until your consciousness is re-integrated into your body. And if your intuitive abilities are not grounded, they can create problems for you on physical, emotional, mental and spiritual levels. Your expansive-yet-unmanaged energy field will unconsciously absorb all kinds of vibrations from your environment – and many of these energetic frequencies will not benefit you.

Not being grounded can lead to many problems, including anxiety, restlessness, depression, poor self-care, accidents, health issues, money problems and, at the most basic level, an inability to manifest your dreams.

If you'll recall our discussion of The Manifestation Matrix, all manifested reality begins as an idea drawn out of the Unified Field. You connect with the Field through your seventh or crown chakra. The energy of an idea drawn out of the Field then runs through the sixth chakra, or third eye center, where the idea begins to present itself as a vision. At the fifth chakra, sound begins to bring the energy of the idea into the realm of form (thus the power of the spoken word). The feeling experience of the idea originates in the heart (fourth chakra) and then creates a very particular vibrational field throughout the body. At the third chakra, the ego takes in this vibrational field as what's true or what it knows. That energy is expressed at the second chakra level in the physical experience of action, choice, behavior – you act in accordance with who you know yourself to be. Finally, at the first chakra level, you project the sum of all these energies into the Ground Consciousness, and that Consciousness is mirrored back to you in the form of your life experiences (you call this "reality.")

This process of the living Manifestation Matrix is almost always happening outside of your awareness. But as you become more aware of your body, it will give you signals that the vibrational essence you are living in and projecting from is out of alignment with where you want to go. When you are disconnected from your body, you are disconnected from those signals. However, when you connect with your body, when you begin to relate to it as the beautiful vehicle for your consciousness that it is, it can support your ability to manifest consciously.

Getting Grounded: Re-Membering Your Body

The grounding exercise built in to the beginning of The Manifestation Matrix Meditation is one way to begin re-building your conscious connection to your body. In addition to that regular practice, I'd recommend several other activities that will help you reconnect with your physical self:

Spend time in nature. Get outside. Take a walk. Listen to the birds. Hug a tree. Wonder at the stars. Go hiking, or ice skating or float aimlessly on a raft in the middle of a picturesque lake. Lie on the ground. Feel the wind on your face. Smell a flower. Wonder what the frogs and crickets are saying when they sing on a summer night. Stand on the earth with your bare feet and feel your energy extending out into the ground.

Eat slowly and mindfully. Rather than go on a diet or get over-zealous about which foods you should or shouldn't eat, just slow down enough to start paying attention to what truly nourishes your body.

Move your body. And do it with awareness. Dance. Walk. Sing your heart out in the car and the shower. Do yoga or tai chi. Get a big yoga ball and pour your body over the top of it. Belly dance. Roller skate. Stretch. Just move and enjoy it!

Breathe.

Slow down.

Get bodywork. Try massage, Jin Shin Jyutsu, Cranio-Sacral work, Reiki, any sort of body and energy work that will awaken your physical intuition.

Have a soul-retrieval experience. The wisdom of ancient shamanic cultures is being revived by modern teachers. Celtic Shaman Pat Tuholske's soul retrieval work with me was critical in helping me get back into my body. You can find out more about Pat and her work at **elementalearthcamp.com.**

Touch. The United States is a touch-starved society. In many other countries, it is commonplace to see men unabashedly hugging each other, women walking arm-in-arm and playing with each other's hair, couples kissing on the street. Whatever you think of such displays, people who touch each other more have an advantage over those of us who were raised to think that extended physical contact is reserved for sex. Being touched in a positive, appropriate way produces endorphins and stimulates the immune system. So look for ways to give and receive touch more often. Give hugs. Brush a friend's hair. Rub a child's back. Dance cheek to cheek. Ask for a foot massage. Begin touching your own body with more consciousness and care.

Celebrate the changing seasons. Ancient societies were in tune with the natural cycles of greening, growing, harvest and waiting. In the current age most of us are disconnected from the way food arrives at our table and we spend most of our time indoors. Learning about ancient festivals celebrated by indigenous cultures can be a way of reawakening our physical consciousness. Celtic and Native American traditions are popular in North America now because so many of the people who live here have ancestors in those cultures. Do you have any interest in exploring your own cultural history? Who were your ancestors and how did they celebrate the changing seasons?

Sacralize your sexuality. Can you envision sex as an act of faith and blessing? Many ancient cultures believed that conscious sex had healing and creative as well as generative power. The ancient Celts, for instance, encouraged sexual activity especially during their festival of Beltane (summer's beginning). Lovers participated in and celebrated the Divine union by coming together in field and wood, blessing the crops, herds and homes as they gave expression to the life-force pulsing through their bodies. Dancing, singing, feasting and lovemaking not only gave pleasure to the participants, it demonstrated the community's intention to enter into the natural energies of the season in hopes that the joys of Beltane would result in healthy babies and bountiful harvests.

Beltane Longing

The music surrounds me
in my modern mini-van
and not the ancient stone circle
of my imagination.
But as the highway rolls by
beneath my tires
the bodhran and harp
the flute and the fiddle
throb in my feet
and pulse in my belly
until the asphalt breaks open
and I am dancing away
from my silver van
to a ring of power
on a misty green hill
where the old ones live
and anything is possible.

This must be why the Baptists
don't want us to dance:
they know that the drums might
awaken the Bean Sidhe
inside of us all
and if she emerged,
hair flying
arms flailing
feet pounding
mouth screaming,
she would herald the death
of our civilized personas.

We would throw away
our crippling shoes
and rip off
our strangling neckties
and dance barefooted
and bare-chested
until the sun tides
ran in our blood
and we came together
under a full moon to remember
a hundred ways
that lips and hands
can praise creation
in the oldest
dance of all.

©2001, Kimberly Schneider

EXERCISE: Embodiment Meditation

Mary Lou Schneider, **MaryLouSchneider.com**, (who also happens to be my mom), created this exercise and shared it with me.

Create an altar in your home, a space that you can decorate as simply or elaborately as you wish. Use it to honor the change of seasons and the important happenings in your life. For this meditation, place some fresh flowers and a candle on your altar. Having set aside some time for solitude and silence, bow reverently in front of your altar while inhaling the scent of the flowers. Allow the fragrance to enliven your senses.

Light the candle. Move into a comfortable, seated pose. With eyes closed, remember a time in childhood when all your senses were alive to the world and you were bursting with energy. Visualize that child body moving freely and joyously.

Acknowledge your body as a messenger with wonderful insights for you. Begin speaking to your body and ask what you should call her or him. Your body is your soul's home while you reside on earth, and it has a name of its own, separate from your ego identity. Wait expectantly for your

124

body to reveal its insights to you. Spend as much time as you need in a meditative dialogue with your body, asking for just one suggestion on how to nurture it. When you have received the message, promise to take action on it. Thank your body and say goodbye. After you have gently returned to present consciousness, write about the experience. Continue your dialogue whenever you wish, remembering to refer to your body by name. Expect to be surprised by what happens when you access your body's wisdom.

The Cornucopia Method of Manifestation Step IV: Raise Your Vibration

You may recall that early on in the book, we discussed how your life arises out of your level of consciousness, thoughts/beliefs, words, emotions and feelings. At each of these levels of being, you are constantly sending out energetic vibrations. Your reality corresponds to where you bring your attention moment to moment. But what determines where your attention is focused?

Since you come from the Unified Field, also known as the Cornucopia Reality, in theory you ought to have access to any possibility imaginable. And when you consciously reconnect with the Unified Field, like you do while utilizing The Manifestation Matrix Meditation, you might get a glimpse of that. But you probably don't hang out in the Cornucopia Reality all of the time. Sometimes, you might get lost in the appearance of material reality. And, as discussed in earlier sections, even when you are operating out of your Essential Self at a conscious level, you've still got to contend with your Unconscious Limiting Beliefs. Those beliefs draw a box around one little corner of the universe and keep most of your energetic awareness inside of that box. Every time you aim for something larger than what you've known, you run into the edge of the box.

So how do you get a bigger box?

We've already looked at a few steps: assuming responsibility for your own life (deciding), awareness (knowing yourself) and becoming familiar with your body's vibratory language (befriending your body). Now we'll focus on a short cut to life outside the box: taking steps to raise your vibration. By raising your vibration, you have access to a much wider array of experiences and you are likely to enjoy more of the experiences you attract.

Here's some really good news: since you've gotten this far in the book, if you've been actively engaged in the exercises (and I'm SURE that if you haven't, you're going to go back and do them NOW, right?), your vibrational frequency is already higher than when you started. You've already engaged in some of the activities that raise your vibration naturally.

How do you know when you are resonating at a higher frequency? Here are some signs:

- *You find yourself smiling for no apparent reason.*
- *You have fewer bouts of worry.*
- *You are less irritable.*
- *You are more trusting.*
- *Your thoughts are positive for longer and longer periods of time.*
- *You are noticing more synchronicities – acausal occurrences that seem to support your intention to grow, expand, create and be happy.*
- *Your intuition is enhanced.*
- *You think about something you would like to have or experience and it appears in your life.*

These are just a few of the ways you might notice that you're vibrating at a higher rate. Even if you've only noticed a slight improvement at this point, that's progress. There have been times in my own journey when a new awareness even made me feel a little worse for awhile! It was sometimes challenging to take an honest look at how I'd been sabotaging myself. Fortunately, those challenges pass – and quickly too, if you stick with the process. (I promise). So wherever you are, just trust that. Be gentle with yourself.

However you're feeling right now, there are lots of ways to quickly raise your vibration. Before we get to the most important long-term tool, here are several you can begin implementing right away:

JUMP START TOOLS FOR RAISING YOUR VIBRATION:

Take a media fast. If it is too much to wean yourself entirely, consider at least switching off the television news for a week and notice how differently you feel. Ponder the fact that what is newsworthy is decided by media interests that are not likely to be in complete alignment with your values and the reality within which you want to live. While I would never condone closing your heart to the suffering of others, news coverage feeds us constant images of violence and conflict without presenting the issues in a larger context or offering practical ways for us to be part of the solution. Here's what I like to do whenever I hear about someone else's suffering: I find peace, joy, contentment, abundance, forgiveness (whatever would bring relief in that situation) inside of myself. I let that experience fill my whole being, and then I send it out to whoever needs it. I know, I know, you've been taught that the compassionate thing to do is to let your own heart break when you are touched by another's pain. But how does that help anyone? If, every time any of us confronted another's suffering, we moved into a heart space of joy and love, we would always know how best to respond. And the vibration of the whole planet would be raised exponentially.

Food for your mind. Remember the old saying "You are what you eat?" Well, the same thing is true for whatever your mind ingests. You are inundated with input that affects your vibration every day: music, books, magazines and conversation. This is a great opportunity to take charge of what you allow in. Fill your car or home with beautiful music, the sounds of nature or healing silence. Bring fresh flowers into your home or office. When you are sitting in traffic, pop in a CD with an inspirational and thought-provoking author, poet or speaker. Listen to my *Terrible Beauty* audiobook, and also try: Deepak Chopra, John O'Donohue, David Whyte, Eckhart Tolle, Jerry and Esther

Hicks and Dr. Samantha St. Julian (Samantha's CDs are not for driving—use those at home). For more ideas go to **FindsForSeekers.com.**

Spend your time with positive people. Do you want to be more or less like the people who usually surround you? Look for people whose lifestyle and way of being in the world you admire and cultivate relationships with them.

Shake up your routine. Take a new route on your daily commute. Eat at a restaurant you would never have considered before. Enroll in a belly dancing class or take up painting. When you break out of your routine, your brain forms new neural pathways, which means that you have more options. You'll feel more space in your life.

Clean Up Your Environment. Switch to non-toxic options for cleaning your home and body. What's good for the earth is good for you, too, so go green when you can. Add some nutrient-rich whole foods to your daily meals. And don't forget to routinely de-clutter your home and work spaces.

Make Sound Your Ally. You'll recall that the fifth chakra, located at the throat, is the energy center that allows you to express the truth of who you are in this world. Sound begins the process of densing down your dreams so that they can take material form. The ancients believed that "the great sound," the Divine Song, brought reality into being. (That's why the word "universe" means "one song"). Use this awareness to your advantage by singing, toning, chanting, moving beautiful healing sounds through your fifth chakra. Also be mindful of what words you choose. Your words are very powerful; they are an important factor in manifestation. As Florence Scovel Shinn said, "Your word is your wand." Be mindful with the power of your speech. Another important way to access the power of sound is through music. Music can change your mood and raise your vibration almost instantly. Think about the lyrics and melodies that make you want to roll down the window and belt out the songs while the wind blows through your hair. Or music that makes you want to move (put it on and then follow your bliss!) Classical music, especially Baroque and Mozart, can be stimulating and restorative at the same time. Or try Gregorian chant. Create a CD or an iPod library and load it up with your favorite feel-good tunes. Listen to them regularly and especially when you are feeling low or want to get inspired.

Be grateful. Medieval mystic Meister Eckhart wrote, "If the only prayer you ever said was 'thank you,' that would be enough." In every situation, look for one thing about which you can feel true appreciation. This is not an exercise of *I should be grateful for x, y and z*; it's about finding the things you truly appreciate. Keep a gratitude journal. Write down thoughts about what you are grateful for as they occur to you, especially regarding the people closest to you and the situations where you have resentments (sometimes, these are one and the same)! You can refer to your journal when you're struggling to remember anything to feel good about.

Make a "gratitude rolodex." Pick three powerful, positive memories — three times in your life when you felt incredibly grateful, good and happy. Practice bringing yourself into those memories until your whole body resonates with the experience. Call on those memories when you are out of sorts. They will give you the positive feelings you need to face your present-moment situation with clarity and open-heartedness.

Synergia. Synergia is a cutting-edge healing modality created by Dr. Samantha St. Julian **synergia.bz**. Dr. St. Julian drew upon traditional Chinese medicine, applied kinesiology, homeopathy, quantum physics, the power of the Multi-Verse and her own magnificent brain to bring Synergia to life. This work will raise your vibration and heal you at every level of experience. Dr. St. Julian can work by phone and she occasionally travels to teach her healing techniques. Her work has been an important part of my own consciousness expansion and healing.

Meditation: Vibrational Medicine

Of all the methods you could choose to raise your vibrational frequency (and it's best to have lots of tools in your toolbox), one of the most critical is meditation. You already have access to The Manifestation Matrix Meditation and that will prove very useful to you. The Manifestation Matrix Meditation requires you to open your seventh chakra, the Throne of Consciousness. This is MUCH easier to do if you have some simple meditation tools, so I'm going to give you a few. But first let's dispel a few misconceptions you might have about meditation.

You've probably heard meditation helps you become a spiritual, enlightened person, creates peace of mind and leads to better health and happiness. All of these things can and do happen with a regular meditation practice, but they aren't likely to happen right away. In fact, what will probably happen at first is that you don't like what you observe and experience when you sit in the quiet.

You may feel fidgety, anxious, bored or tired. You might start thinking about all the things you have to get done today. You might notice that just underneath that busyness of your normal existence is a feeling of unease. You might uncover pain or anger or a deep sadness with no apparent cause. You might see parts of yourself that make you want to flee.

Why would you EVER want to do this?

Because sitting through those feelings is the road to self-compassion and freedom. The real point of a meditation session, especially at the beginning, is not peace of mind. If you don't realize this when you start meditating, you will think that there must be something wrong with you. You will likely become discouraged and quit. The real purpose of meditation is mindtraining, or the development of mindfulness.

Mindfulness is the quality of presence or awareness that a person brings into lived experience — it is the ability to view your thoughts and actions and the behaviors of other people from the perspective of a witness rather than a reactor. As a witness, you empower yourself to make conscious choices rather than reacting out of habitual patterns.

Meditation leads to mindfulness.

And mindfulness creates a space within which you can break free from your limiting beliefs, harmful habits and compulsive reactions. Along the way, you are naturally creating health, happiness and peace of mind.

Meditation Basics

There's a reason that some form of meditation has been a part of every great religious tradition. Behaviors and attitudes all begin in the mind, in your conscious and unconscious thoughts and beliefs. Mahatma Gandhi observed:

Your beliefs become your thoughts
your thoughts become your words
your words become your actions
your actions become your habits
your habits become your values
and your values become your destiny.

Meditation allows you to observe your mind. As soon as you become an observer, or witness, you recognize that you are not your mind. You are not your beliefs. Your mind is a fantastic tool. It does not define you. When you realize this you gain the power to change your mind. And when you change your mind, you change your life.

Meditation, or mindtraining, is the surest, smoothest path to transformation. That's why The Manifestation Matrix Meditation is the foundation of The Cornucopia Method of Manifestation.

It's the regular discipline of meditation that produces results. Just as you can't sit on the couch for six days and then work out for two hours one day a week and expect satisfactory change, the greatest benefits of meditation come when you do it daily. It helps if you do your meditation at roughly the same time each day. Morning works well for many people, for a few reasons.

First, if you make it a habit to meditate before you do anything else, you're more likely to do it. If you put off your meditation until later, as the day wears on you will probably get pulled into your busyness and forget about meditating or make excuses for why you can't do it. Second, meditating right when you wake up gives you easier access to your unconscious mind so you can bring about change more quickly. Finally, morning meditation sets the tone for your day, preparing you to face each moment with more clarity and creativity.

Evening is also a nice time to meditate, putting your mind in a relaxed state for sleep. However, when you meditate late in the day, it's easier to forget or just fall asleep. So if you want to meditate at night, consider your evening meditation a supplement rather than a substitute for a morning practice.

Meditation will go better for you if you find a place in your home where you'll be undisturbed. With two children living at home, it can be a challenge for me to find a quiet, uncluttered space to meditate. But I make a special point to keep one room neat and organized. This is where I pray and meditate (usually a few minutes before my children wake, but they know to come in quietly if I'm meditating. My youngest often sits in my lap).

If you don't have a room to claim for meditation, stake out a special corner. Clear off a shelf or a corner of a dresser and place a candle or sacred object there to mark it as special. Over time, if you meditate in the same place each day, you will notice your whole system relax as soon as you enter that room.

Many meditation experts will tell you to meditate for thirty minutes a day. I used to recommend this. However, most of my clients have been women with many different people and projects pulling at them, so my suggestions to set aside thirty minutes a day for meditation were typically met with disbelief or laughter. Looking at my own life, I realized my clients were on to something. So I switched to a plea for five minutes.

Give yourself five minutes a day. If you can't commit to that, go for sixty seconds. Or even thirty seconds. I don't know anyone who can seriously claim she or he is unable to wake up thirty seconds earlier for meditation. That's how I had to start — just a few seconds each day, then a few minutes. Now I wake up early enough to do thirty minutes most mornings because I have experienced for myself how meditation transforms every moment of my life.

Your thirty minutes may come later. But start where you are. Thirty seconds a day, for now.

The Easiest Way to Meditate

As you've no doubt discovered if you've been experimenting with meditation, the process is not exactly easy! It can seem as if everything and everyone (especially your own mind) is conspiring to keep you from finding the stillness you seek.

I read a great article once in *Spirituality and Health* magazine about a woman who went all the way to Tibet and hiked up a mountain in order to find the ultimate meditation place. She believed her life at home was too hectic for her to have a great meditation experience. In Tibet, she knew she would find peace of mind. But when she reached her destination, someone else was on the mountain making unbelievable amounts of noise. It was so irritating! Here she had spent all of this time and money and energy to find the perfect place that would allow the silence within her to emerge, only to be foiled by someone else. And yet, in the midst of her outrage, she finally got it:

Meditation is not about pushing the world away to find the perfect peaceful place. Meditation is about learning to create peace in your own mind regardless of what the world is doing.

I have to tell you, this was a relief for me to read and also a wakeup call. As a busy wife and mother of two children, it was easy for me to make excuses not to meditate. There wasn't time, and there certainly wasn't an abundance of quiet in my home. After reading the aforementioned article, however, I had no more excuses. But I still wasn't sure how to accomplish a daily disciplined practice of meditation.

I tried movement as meditation: tai chi, yoga, walking meditation, mudras. Since I have a hard time sitting still, these methods were easier for me than a traditional practice of sitting and emptying my mind; however, I still didn't make the time on a regular basis.

The real breakthrough in my personal meditation practice came when my mom introduced me to the writings of Eknath Easwaran. Sri Easwaran was born in India and raised in the Hindu tradition, yet he was also educated in Western religions and had a deep respect for Christian mysticism, Buddhism and all the sacred literature of the world. He came to the U.S. in the 1960s and established the first accredited course in America on meditation (at Berkley University).

Sri Easwaran created a non-denominational, non-sectarian, Eight Point Program for actualizing human potential. **Easwaran.org.** The first two points of his Eight Point Program are silent repetition of the Holy Name, or mantram, throughout the day (addressed later in this chapter) and meditation by silent repetition of memorized, inspirational passages from the world's great mystics and scriptures.

Meditating on a sacred text has an almost miraculous power to still the mind and the body. Slowly, silently repeating the words of a sacred text gives the mind something to do. It's too busy to worry about what to make for dinner or who you forgot to call or whether your friend is mad at you or where you might have left that library book. And it's busy with something wholesome and nourishing—real soul food!

As you repeat the same prayers or poems in your mind every day for weeks and weeks during your meditation time, it begins to alter you at a subconscious level. Without having to think so much about how to be peaceful or happy, you become more peaceful and happy. It is a natural result of marinating your mind in the sweet juices of the sacred.

The first few times you meditate with whatever inspirational passage you choose, you will be focused on memorizing—reading the words and then closing your eyes to silently repeat a few lines at a time. That's okay. Eventually the words will seep into your mind and then come to you naturally, and not just when you are meditating. The healing words will even cradle you while you sleep. You may find that when you wake up in the middle of the night or in the morning, the first line of one of these sacred texts will pop into your head.

EXERCISE:

Pick one of the Jump Start Tools for raising your vibration (listed earlier in this chapter) and implement it right away. In addition, continue with the regular practice of The Manifestation Matrix Meditation. Once you are doing both of those activities on a regular basis, begin reviewing sacred literature. You might consider mystical poets like Hafiz, Rumi or Lalla or a scriptural passage from your own spiritual tradition. Eknath Easwaran's wonderful book, *Timeless Wisdom: Passages for Meditation from the World's*

Saints and Sages, includes beautiful selections from various traditions. Choose a passage, prayer or poem that speaks to you. Spend a few minutes with it every day until you have it memorized. Then commit yourself to meditating with the passage each morning, even if you begin with thirty-second intervals. At this point, consistency is more important than length of time. If you already have a regular habit of meditation, add sacred literature to your practice. Eventually you may want to memorize more passages to lengthen your meditation time.

After a few weeks of daily meditation, slowly begin integrating the other suggestions for raising your vibration. You may feel like you want to do everything at once, but you are more likely to stick with the changes if you take them slowly. Be gentle with yourself. You created your habits over a lifetime. You'll be able to release them more easily if you do one new thing at a time. Additionally, as you deepen into your meditation practice, you may find that some of your old routines will fall away naturally.

Remember to write in your journal about the changes you are making in your life. Write about what you notice. What has come easily? What has been challenging? Do you see any patterns in the way your ego responds to your new routines? Becoming familiar with those patterns is part of knowing yourself. After awhile when you notice the patterns you'll smile and say, "Ah, there you are again!" When that happens, you have the power to make a conscious choice instead of reacting out of an Unconscious Limiting Belief. You are in the moment. You're in touch with Essence.

The Cornucopia Method of Manifestation Step V: Be Here Now

There exists only the present instant... a Now which always and without end is itself new. There is no yesterday nor any tomorrow, but only Now...
- Meister Eckhart, Christian mystic of the Middle Ages

The last step of The Cornucopia Method of Manifestation is a natural extension of the first four. By deciding to take responsibility for your life, knowing yourself, befriending your body and raising your vibration, you are already more capable of being present.

Time and space are concepts created for living in the material world. They are necessary features of a physical experience; however, they separate us from our source. That's why the only way to connect with Essence is to step outside of time and space: to step into the space between thoughts, as we discussed in the Mechanics of Manifestation.

Your power is in the present moment. That's where you will find inspiration, creativity, peace and all the resources you need to respond beautifully, in that moment. Now is where you remember who you are.

In any given moment, there are only two important questions to ask yourself:

Who do I want to be, right now, in this moment? and

What would that person do, right now?

Sometimes the answer to the second question will be: *nothing.*

Or the honest answer might be: *I have no idea.* So then your next step becomes to look for new reference points, examples of other people whose ways of living inspire you.

But often, just by bringing your whole self into the moment, an inspired answer will bubble up inside you. And you'll know.

The trick is to remember to be conscious enough to stop and ask yourself those two questions, especially in times of stress. To remember to be in the moment. When you can do that, you will be open to inspiration. And when you are fully in the present moment, unfettered by past stories or worries about the future, you have whatever you need to ACT on that inspiration. Inspired action creates magic and miracles. That's how your dreams become reality.

Inspired Action Creates Magic and Miracles

You likely know the story of Moses parting the Red Sea. Maybe you even have the Cecil B. DeMille image implanted in your head from the epic movie *The Ten Commandments*: Charlton Heston, as Moses, holding his staff up in the air as the Israelites escape the Egyptians through the miraculous path in the sea. But you may not know the whole story of the Red Sea parting. It's a story of inspired action creating magic and miracles. And I learned about it when I needed a miracle.

In April of 2005, David and I received some difficult news about Bridget's heart. She'd already had three open-heart surgeries and now her aortic valve was failing due to a thickening of the tissue beneath it. At the age of five, her heart was still growing rapidly, and her cardiologist was concerned that a valve replacement at this critical time might mean multiple surgeries over the coming year as her heart outgrew the new valves. He was not enthusiastic about the outcome of an imminent surgical intervention, but neither could he offer us any medical alternatives. Her heart couldn't wait. We were going in every few weeks to check the pressure gradient over the valve and it was rising rapidly.

We left the doctor's office in a daze. The next step was to consult with Bridget's surgeon and set a date for the procedure.

I couldn't shake off my sense of dread about the surgery. It had always been a scary prospect, but this time it felt wrong in every way. What choice did we have though? I was talking about our quandary with my friend Rachel, a student of Kabbalah (an ancient philosophy associated with Hebrew mystical teachings), who wisely said to me, "When what you know is not helpful, uncertainty becomes your friend."

The next day I received an email from another friend offering a Kabbalistic interpretation of the Red Sea story. Imagine this scene:

The Israelites have fled Egypt but now are trapped at the shoreline of the Red Sea with Pharaoh's troops in pursuit. Moses calls out to God for help.

God says to Moses, "Moses, why are you asking me? You have what you need. I have given you the power. Walk through the sea."

So, Moses raises his staff.

Nothing happens.

Moses keeps his arm raised. He tells the people to begin walking into the water. They do.

Nothing happens.

People begin to wail as Pharaoh's chariots appear on the horizon.

Nothing happens.

Moses' staff remains aloft. One faith-filled soul keeps walking. He walks until the water reaches his knees, his hips, his chest, his shoulders. He tastes the salty fluid in his mouth. He walks until the sea reaches his nose—

And the sea parts.

God gives us the power to create miracles. And we manifest those miracles when we act on our inspiration.

The story gave me hope. All was not lost. I just needed to walk into the water. But what was the water, for me? For Bridget? What was the next step? Every day I walked and prayed and cried and let go, wanting answers. Wanting to do something. Knowing that there was nothing to do but be present. And wait for inspiration.

That week I had an appointment to receive bodywork. During the treatment I went into a state between sleeping and waking that was somewhat like a dream. I had a vision of Bridget on the operating table. In the vision, I watched her die. I was inconsolable, not only because we had lost our dear girl, but because I had allowed the surgery to go forward, knowing all along that it was not the answer for her.

My witness Self watched and asked "Was there any other choice?" I turned my back on the operating room and saw nothing but dense gray fog. The Unknown beckoned. I didn't know what it held. I only knew I was not satisfied with the only clear possibility before me. So I walked into the mist.

I couldn't see the path beneath my feet. I didn't know where to go, so I stopped. I waited in the silence, the nothingness, for what may have been a few moments or many minutes. It felt like a long time.

Out of the corner of my right eye I saw a very small, brilliant and sparkling golden light. It hovered for a short time and then began moving away. I followed. I awoke, knowing that there was another possibility for Bridget. I just didn't know what it was.

After my bodywork session I called David from my car.

"Where are you?" I asked.

"At the corner of Delmar and Big Bend. I was thinking about grabbing some lunch."

Ironically, that was just around the corner from the parking lot where I was sitting.

"Let's eat together then," I told him. "We need to talk."

Over lunch I told David about the vision and explained that I didn't want Bridget to have the surgery. "All right. What do we do instead then?"

I still didn't know. I felt as if we needed to leave the country. But where to go? Lourdes? Some cutting-edge doctor in Europe? I didn't have any answers, and the clock was ticking.

When I got home I called our friend Samantha, who happens to be clairvoyant (tip of the day: get some psychic friends. They come in handy). After I shared my vision and my feeling about leaving the U.S., Samantha said, "Brazil popped into my head. But I have no idea why."

So I went to Google. And I typed in these words: *healer Brazil.*

Immediately I pulled up dozens of websites about Joao Teixeira de Faria, a medium healer in the little village Abadiania in the Brazilian hill country. One site said, "Joao is known to be the most gifted healer in the last 2,000 years." Wow. The most gifted healer since Jesus (at least according to this website) happened to be alive now — and he lived in Brazil?

You'd better believe I was paying attention. I'd never heard of this guy, but I was seriously interested. I spent the next several hours reading story after story of miraculous healings attributed to de Faria, popularly known as "John of God." (Incidentally, Joao has since become quite famous since being discovered by Oprah, network TV news and The Omega Institute, but in 2005 he was not well known in the U.S.)

By the time David got home, I was ready to go. I told him about John of God and showed him some of the websites.

"So, what do you think?" I asked.

"About what?"

"About this! About John of God. About going to Brazil."

Silence.

More silence.

"Let me get this straight. You want to take our family, including our daughter who needs heart surgery and doesn't walk, to a developing country where we know no one and don't speak the language, to see a guy who has a fourth grade education and speaks no English, because your psychic friend Samantha said there might be something in Brazil?"

"Yes. That's exactly what I'm saying."

David left the room.

Over the next few days, I continued to bring it up. He continued to ignore me, hoping, I suppose, that this idea would be replaced by something a bit less reckless.

Day after day I received more signs that Brazil was the right choice, but David seemed to be unmoved.

I didn't want to take Bridget to Brazil by myself. So on a Wednesday morning I had a little talk with St. Joseph. He's the patron saint of working fathers and I hoped he could help us. "Listen Joseph, I can't do this alone. If this trip is really the best thing for Bridget, then you need to give David some kind of sign. Show him."

A couple of hours later, David called me in tears.

"I told my bosses I needed a couple of weeks off to go to Brazil."

I was stunned. When he had left that morning he'd asked me to stop bugging him about it.

"Fifteen minutes after I told them, they called me into Senior's office. They want to buy plane tickets. For all four of us. $4,500."

So, David got his sign.

Four weeks later we were on a plane to Brazil.

As soon as we decided to go, it seemed we had stepped into a new reality. David and I both felt that the healing energies of Brazil were working to prepare us for the trip. When we got there and saw the stars of the Southern Hemisphere twinkling above us, they confirmed our feeling that we'd entered a parallel universe. We had created a new possibility for Bridget and for ourselves.

While we were in Brazil, we experienced miracles large and small. Healings of old griefs. Deep connections with new friends. Bridget learned to walk within twenty-four hours of receiving an invisible surgery. And, of course, we wondered: what about her heart?

When we got back to the states, Bridget had an echocardiogram.

Her heart had apparently not improved. In fact, it was a little worse. Even though we'd heard in Abadiania again and again that healing takes many forms, that the healing was offered only as a way to bring people closer to God, we were disappointed. We had been hoping for an instant miracle. We wanted her heart to be healed.

We knew the next thing the doctor would say: surgery, right away. But he surprised us.

"I know what the echocardiogram shows, but I also know what I'm seeing with my eyes. This is a different child than the one I saw before you went to Brazil. I don't think I'm feeling this just because I know where you've been. Let's not schedule the surgery yet. Come back in a few weeks and we'll do one more echo."

So, that's what we did.

And, when we went back, her heart was a little better.

A few weeks later, it had stabilized.

We were able to postpone the surgery for almost a year. Right before the procedure I had another vision. The little golden light I'd seen in the gray fog of my vision became hundreds of golden lights. They were the healing energies of Abadiania. They flowed through the operating and recovery rooms. I knew that Bridget would be all right. And by the time she had the surgery, her heart had grown enough to accept an adult-sized valve. We'd gotten her through the critical period of growth that had so worried her doctor. The Red Sea had parted. And we walked safely through it to a new reality on the other side.

Parting Your Own Red Sea

Inspired action creates magic and miracles because it is the perfect marriage of Divine intervention and personal responsibility. It allows you to be who you are: God in Action — the Divine Made Manifest.

Your job is to be present. Show up. Be conscious. Look for inspiration and act on it.

Note that your job description says nothing about getting every detail of the road ahead. You don't get a blow-by-blow plan. You get some crazy instruction like, "Okay, Moses, lead the Israelites out of Egypt with whatever they can carry on their backs." And then you go. You don't wait for tools to build a bridge over the Red Sea before you take off, nor do you receive any indication of how the apparent obstacles will be dealt with when you confront them. You will, however, want some tools and rules for the road. For instance, the mindtraining you'll be developing in your daily meditation practice will strengthen your ability to be present. A daily meditation routine, even if you're starting out with thirty seconds at a time, is like putting money in the bank every day. When you need the money, it's there for you.

In addition to your daily morning practice, there are a few things you can do on the go. They are tools for real life that will help you step out of the past, the future and your storylines and into the reality of the moment. My favorite "be here now" tool is the mantram.

Mantram: An On-the-Go Tool for Present-Moment Living

Just as meditation on an inspirational poem or sacred text gives the mind something to do during meditation, you can quiet your mind and bring it back to the present throughout your day by focusing on a sacred word.

It doesn't matter whether you have an affinity for a particular religious tradition, or even if you consider yourself a spiritual person. When you meditate with a sacred word or phrase that arises out of a long-standing tradition, you connect energetically with the thousands of people throughout the years who have focused on that sacred word. You now have the power to pull your mind out of its old patterns—it's like jumping on the Collective Super Highway of neural energy! Sometimes you need something that powerful to pull your mind off of its habitual hamster wheel.

In Part One, I introduced the concept of the mantram as a tool to use during The Manifestation Matrix Meditation and I listed some possible choices, including Allah, Jesus, Lord, Krishna and Ave Maria. Some other examples of sacred words and phrases that work well as mantrams are: Barukh attah Adonai, Allah, Om Mani Padme Hum, Ave Maria, or Rama (Gandhi's mantram—it means "joy" or "rejoicing" in Sanskrit). My own personal mantram is "I AM."

Consider your phrase carefully as it will build in power over time. You don't want to keep changing your sacred word or it will not have the long-term impact of a well-chosen, oft-returned-to mantram. If you use a mantram regularly, it will be like a boat that carries you gracefully over the choppy waters of life.

When do you use your mantram? Anytime your mind is free. And anytime you find yourself caught in a storyline. Do you experience impatience while in a long line at the store? Are you ever angry about another person's behavior? Are you occasionally overwhelmed? Do you ever feel like someone you love has let you down? Are you sometimes ashamed of your own behavior? The answer to those questions, of course, is yes. We all have those feelings. And they arise from the stories our minds make up about our lives. Those stories pull us out of the power of the present moment and into mental gyrations that can tie us up in knots.

In the past when you felt such emotions arising, you probably allowed them to sweep you away into minutes or hours of self-inflicted misery. With the mantram, however, every inner experience, from boredom to despair, from

146

irritation to rage, becomes an opportunity to discover within yourself what the Bhagavad Gita calls "the peace in which all sorrows end." As you call upon the Holy Name, you are calling the Divine into your life moment to moment. You are reminding yourself of your true nature. In a sense, each time your inner voice speaks the mantram you are clearing out the clutter and opening a healing space in your mind.

Next time you find yourself waiting, doing a household chore, walking or engaging in any mindless activity, turn inward. Begin silently repeating your mantram. If you find yourself struggling to fall asleep, reach for your mantram instead of sleeping tablets. When you are tempted to send off an angry note or email to someone, get out your journal and write your mantram fifty times. When you think your partner or child is going to send you over the edge, head outside and take a brisk walk, repeating the mantram with each step.

The mantram sweeps away the mazes in your mind so that the power of your Presence, your Essential Self, wells up within you. It returns you to the moment. It calls your attention to what really matters. The mantram reminds you that you are more than your volatile emotions. It opens your heart to the truth that each one of us, every messy and imperfect person on the planet, belongs to one family — the family of God. The family of Essence.

You never know when the next occasion will arise to disturb your inner peace (perhaps you won't have to wait long!), but using the mantram is a fast and easy way to come back to the peace and truth that is always available when you bring your full self to the present. With the mantram, you can meditate throughout the day without ever sitting down!

If you would like to delve more deeply into the potential of the mantram or sacred word to transform your life, my favorite books on this subject are *The Mantram Handbook* and *Passage Meditation* by Eknath Easwaran.

Slow Down

Most people are in a hurry.

Do you ever rush around for no apparent reason? Say "hurry up" to your children? Cram so much into each hour that you are consistently hurried and late for appointments? Are you aggravated on the road when you end up behind a slow vehicle or you encounter an accident or construction?

Living in a state of constant hurriedness has negative ramifications on your body as well as your mind. Your adrenal glands go into overdrive and your body produces chemicals appropriate to a fight-or-flight situation every day. You might feel constantly tired but have difficulty sleeping, or wake up exhausted no matter how much sleep you get.

If those symptoms are familiar to you, then your body is sending you a message. It's telling you to slow down. Take a breath. Step into the space between your thoughts. Bring your full presence and attention to whatever you are doing. If you are eating, eat. If you are working, work. If you are spending some free time with a loved one, be with him or her. Notice what you are feeling. Take in what your companion is saying; notice facial expressions, body language, emotional content. Be present.

When you bring your attention to slowing down, you become more present to every moment. That sensation that life is passing you by will gently fade away as you show up for each experience, bringing your full self with you.

JUMP START TOOLS FOR SLOWING DOWN:

Here are some simple ways to help you slow down and Be Here Now:

Choose a mantram and repeat it quietly inside your mind anytime you are distressed, agitated or engaged in an activity that does not require you to think. In this way, you sharpen your mind to be an effective tool you can pull out when you need it, instead of an extension of your ego that runs on autopilot.

Shed all pretenses and live authentically. When you concentrate on being true to your Self instead of acting out of a role, you'll have to slow down enough to remember who you really are.

When you find yourself hurrying, take a deep breath. Stop.

Leave a little bit early for every appointment so you'll have time to drive the speed limit — then you won't need to worry about a little bit of traffic.

Notice your breathing. Shallow breathing usually occurs when you're in a state of hurriedness. Breathe fully and deeply, bringing oxygen to your whole body.

Take a look at your daily to-do list and cut it in half. After awhile, when you are making those to-do lists you can be more realistic about what you'll get done and also leave time and space to breathe and be open to surprises. I often decline invitations or space social engagements so that I don't have too many things booked in one week. And I've dropped many of the committees, groups and other ongoing commitments that used to swallow my time. As you become more comfortable with being present, you may find you wish to let go of some of the activities you once thought necessary to your life. (Hint: you probably won't miss them. And if you do find that something you've released brought more to your life than you realized, you can choose it again with consciousness and joy).

Read Eknath Easwaran's book, *Take Your Time*, or listen to Eckhart Tolle's *The Power of Now* to inspire you as you practice slowing down.

Are We There Yet?

Congratulations! You're now familiar with all five steps of The Cornucopia Method of Manifestation. Let's review them one more time:

I. **Decide**
II. **Know Yourself**
III. **Befriend Your Body**
IV. **Raise Your Vibration**
V. **Be Here Now**

So you've worked your way through all five steps. And you know how to do The Manifestation Matrix Meditation. You might be asking yourself: "Are we there yet? Am I complete? Is there life after transformation?"

Here's a little secret about the quest for transformation: There's no end to it.

Maybe you already know this. You understand that it's all about the journey. But deep down, do you really believe it? Isn't there some part of you that just wants to reach the summit, find Nirvana or, as my Grandma used to say, sing with the choirs of angels in heaven?

I know that many, many years into my own spiritual journey I was still searching for the answer that would keep me immune from pain. Sometimes I still catch myself falling into that Unconscious Limiting Belief. The desire to be free of pain must be wired into human beings, for there is some response to it in every spiritual tradition from the Eleusinian Mysteries to Christianity to Islam: The Way. The Way to Inner Peace. The Way to Joy. The Way to live forever. This is what we take on faith.

And then at some point we reach a crossroads. Something terrible and unexpected takes our breath away. Or we have an experience that just makes no sense within our current paradigm. Everything we've begun to believe is now called into question.

This is the choice point.

This is the time when we realize that perhaps we were searching for The Answer. And now that something painful or confusing is happening, we are ready to dismiss this most recent answer in a series of discarded answers and look for the next one. Or retreat into an older way of thinking that seems more secure in the face of current challenges.

This is the place where most people give up on their big dreams. They become lost in the appearance of loss and scarcity. They think to themselves, *It was never meant to be anyway. I knew it was too good to be true.*

All the great metaphysical teachers talk about how to navigate through these periods of challenge. Florence Scovel Shinn stated that before a "big demonstration" (a conscious manifestation that takes a person into a new experience of who they are), everything seems to go wrong. This is happening because old patterns are emerging to be healed. When you are in the middle of such an experience, though, it might be hard to remember that healing is happening, or that everything you need is right here. You might even feel like your house is on fire.

House on Fire

Your house
is on fire.

Quick—
what will you take
with you
into that new
life,
the one
you hadn't planned?

The one without
the layers
of meaning
and belief,
carelessly constructed yet
protected
with such
blind
tenacity?

Choose now—
will you keep
your relationships
as you've known them?

Your ways of being
in the world?

Will you crawl out
of the house
at last,
gasping for clean air,
having risked it all
for one memento
of the person
you used to be?

Arrogant presumption,
this pretense of choosing.

As if the Soul,
having sought
its ego-erasing crucible
would now empower
your illusions
of control.

Why keep running
back
into the wreckage?

Better to surrender
wholeheartedly.

Let the flames
take it all—even
your blueprint
for life after immolation.

Trust in the miracle
beyond your designing:

The post-surrender peace
that comes
from somehow knowing
amidst the ashes
you'll find the treasure
that was always hiding
beneath your dross,
waiting for one more fire
to set it free.

©2011, Kimberly V. Schneider

When your house is on fire, when old patterns surface, it may seem like all is lost. That's when it is most important to remember your vision and act in the certainty that all is well, no matter how things appear.

Napoleon Hill attributed the discouraging experiences that often precede the realization of your dreams to a hidden guide. The role of the hidden guide is to create persistence tests, which act as a gateway to the realm of success. It is by passing through these persistence tests that you become more fully conscious of your power to manifest, because you gain the lived experience of acting in accordance with your vision rather than your history or your circumstances.

Hill advised his readers to cultivate persistence through: 1) clarity of purpose combined with a burning desire to achieve that purpose, 2) a definite plan expressed through continuous action, 3) a mind tightly closed against all negative and discouraging influences and 4) an alliance with one or more people who encourage follow-through.

Having worked your way through the five steps of The Cornucopia Method of Manifestation, next time you reach a choice point—a place of challenge—you will recognize your desire to avoid that challenge as a distraction. You will realize that the only answer you need is the one that will come to you when you show up entirely for whatever is happening right now.

Your ego won't stop trying to protect Unconscious Limiting Beliefs. And you won't get through all of the old patterns that need to be healed because you'll never be done growing. There's always more, remember? Each time you expand, you'll need to let go of the way you used to be. So no matter how many stories you release, there will be more layers to go. But it doesn't have to be excruciating. When you can approach your challenges with a sense of adventure instead of resistance, life is much easier (and more fun!)

Buddhist nun Pema Chodron, author and teacher of Tonglen meditation, tells a wonderful story of the man who brought Tonglen from India to Tibet. Legend says this man was so far along the road to enlightenment that he was afraid Tibet would not offer him enough ego challenges. He had heard that the Tibetan people were so easy to get along with, he worried he wouldn't find anyone there to trigger his ego and help him uncover his resistance. So he sought out a traveling companion, a thoroughly disagreeable boy whom he paid to serve him his tea. In this way he sought to insure his continued spiritual progress. Once he reached Tibet, however, he discovered that he need not have brought the disagreeable tea boy after all. The Tibetan people offered plenty of opportunities for his growth!

This story always makes me smile and gives me hope. It reminds me that I don't need to be perfect. In fact, it's a sweet way of cautioning me against that feeling of having arrived. If I stay there for too long, my Essential Self will be sure to throw me a situation to shake me up. And then my ego will certainly react. Another illusion shattered!

I can't promise you an easy life just because you know The Cornucopia Method of Manifestation. But you do have tools now that will make your journey a little gentler and more enjoyable. And I can also give you some clues about how to recognize when your ego has taken over. In the next section, we'll explore the four most common obstacles to conscious manifestation, how to recognize them, and what to do when they arise.

Part Three

Trouble in Paradise: Recognizing the Four Most Common Obstacles to Conscious Manifestation

*#/%! I Did it Again!

The Four Attitudes that Block Magic and Miracles

Your ego can sabotage conscious manifestation in many creative ways, but they all boil down to Four Limiting Attitudes that will likely keep you on your toes for as long as you're alive:

- o Resistance
- o Judgment
- o Guilt and Blame
- o Pretending

All of the attitudes are related, but I am separating them for the purpose of discussion to make them easier to understand.

Let's be clear about one thing: EVERYONE encounters life situations that trigger these attitudes and NO ONE is immune to them. They are part of our human condition. There is a difference, however, between people who are often frustrated and people whose lives seem to move along with joy and ease. The second group is more conscious of the Four Limiting Attitudes and is therefore not a slave to them. The goal of a conscious manifester is to be aware of the attitudes and to catch them as they arise most of the time.

As you read through the explanations of the Four Limiting Attitudes and how they inhibit conscious manifestation, see if you can think of examples from your own life.

Limiting Attitude #1: Resistance

Resistance is pushing against what is and making up a story that things should be different. This is the biggest obstacle to conscious manifestation.

When you are in resistance, you might not even be aware that you're resisting. You might not be aware that you're making up a story at all, because the first and most important form of resistance is typically unconscious: *resistance to the very idea that you are responsible for creating your own reality.* That's why it's so easy to look outside yourself (the economy, your family, your boss, your physical limitations, etc.) as the cause of whatever is wrong in your life.

For instance, if you are struggling financially, resistance might take the form of being angry with politicians, the government, your employer, your clients, people who owe you money or people who have more money than you have. Or maybe you worry about whether you will have money to pay your bills next week, or send your child to college next year. Society would tell you that these sorts of worries are not resistance at all, that they are responsible reactions to a limited financial situation. But it is your resistance — your belief that you should have more money than you have right now — that is creating your sufferingand your feeling of lack.

Consider: Is the act of worrying a truly responsible choice? Are feeding fear and anger optimal reactions to a perception of lack? How does worry support your ability to respond in this moment? Does your fear bring clarity? Does your anger make you a better problem solver? The external situation of a perceived financial lack is not creating your reality. Your stories about what the amount of money you have right now and your emotional responses to those stories are creating your internal reality. And when your story includes an assumption that *things should not be this way*, then you will attract more experiences that you believe are not what they should be.

A common misperception about the Law of Attraction is that once you start understanding the principles behind it, you'll never have any challenges. That's because when you get down to the essence of what most people are looking for in any sort of spiritual, religious or philosophical idea, it's to avoid pain. So I've had clients who come away from watching a popular movie or reading a book about manifestation thinking, *If I can just figure out the right way to do everything, then I'm never again going to have pain in my life. I'm never again going to have frustration. I'm never again going to suffer an ego disappointment.*

Freedom from challenge is not what we're going for here. In fact, the suffering you're usually doing your best to avoid does not really come from the challenge at all, but from your resistance to the challenge. There's going to be some pain in life, there's going to be frustration, there's going to be disappointment. That's natural. Law of Attraction experts Esther and Jerry Hicks call challenging experiences "contrast" — those things you need to experience in order to become more and more clear about what you want to create. And as we discussed in the previous section, when you are expanding your consciousness, you will often experience old, painful patterns *on your way to transcending them*. So challenging situations are not the problem. The real problem is your resistance.

Resistance to what you are experiencing in the moment actually pushes what you say you want farther and farther away from you.

How can this be? Because when you are in resistance, you are in the energetic vibration of *My life is not working. I don't have what I want.* That's what you are projecting, and so that's what you draw to yourself.

Everything you manifest in your life, every single experience you bring into form, contains a gift for you.

Within every perceived problem is a solution. Within every perceived nightmare is a doorway to your dreams. The situations you experience as difficulties are actually like stepping stones that can bring you closer to what you desire. But only if you recognize them as such.

Unfortunately, you probably never learned to do this. More likely, instead of walking right up to those stepping-stones and using them to cross over your turbulent times, you've raised your fists at them and told them that they shouldn't be there (or even run in the opposite direction). So, in essence, resistance is saying to the Universe: "I don't want to have this experience of challenge. It shouldn't be happening. I don't want to get clear about what I want so I can fully face and participate in this experience. I don't like it. I'm going to run away from it or fight it instead."

But then you keep saying to the Universe: *Hey, what I really want is xyz!!! When are you going to give me what I need to get there?* And then, when the experience comes along that will show you exactly what you need to learn to move closer to your desires, you think it's a punishment, a curse, bad luck or someone out to get you. And you say again, *I don't like this!* When you resist the learning opportunity, you are really resisting what you say you want.

Let's look at a hypothetical example.

Pretend for a moment that your heart's desire is to drive a Ferrari on the Autobahn in Germany. You don't have the car yet, you have no passport, you've never been on an airplane and you don't even know how to drive. But in your wildest dreams, the sun is shining on you in the driver's seat of your red Italian convertible and you are flying down the road in complete and joyous control of that vehicle, the wind is whipping through your hair and there's no other car in sight to slow you down.

There are a lot of things you'll need to do and learn in order to realize your dream. But what if every time you get into the seven-year-old Ford the driving school uses to train its students, you say to yourself, *I shouldn't be driving a rusty old Ford! I need to be in a Ferrari! This is terrible! I hate Fords! I hate rust! I need new leather and Ferrari red! I'm not going to drive this car!*

What will happen is that you'll never learn to drive. Similarly, if you tell yourself each time you are standing in line to apply for a passport for your trip to Germany, *I shouldn't be standing here in a dingy government office; I should be flying free down the Autobahn,* and you become so disgusted with standing in line that you leave without getting your application, then you will never get the passport, and you will never leave the country.

You might be thinking that this is a ridiculous example, because if you really wanted to drive on the Autobahn you wouldn't give up on your dream just because you had to drive a junky car or wait in line for a passport. And you're probably right; you wouldn't. But that's because in this example, the steps you need to take are clearly defined. You know what you need to do to realize your goal. The unpleasantries you would encounter in this situation are easily recognizable steps along the way to your destination. But in real life, the opportunities to move closer to what you desire are rarely so obvious. They come disguised as situations and people you'd rather avoid. So you miss them, or run away from them or retaliate against them and wonder why your life is so hard.

Look at what you've been resisting in your own life. Is something causing you pain or hardship? Stop telling yourself that it shouldn't be happening. Wherever you are right now, whatever you're experiencing, it's exactly what you need in order to get you where you want to go...but your experience can only take you toward your desire if you step right into it and get the lesson.

EXERCISE:

Think of one situation in the past that was extremely difficult for you, but now that it is over, you are in a much better place because of how it changed you. Perhaps you learned something or changed your mind about something. Maybe you do things differently now. Could you have

161

experienced that same transformation in any other way? **Write about your insights in your journal.**

What's Up with Resistance Anyway?

If resistance is so counterproductive, then why do we engage in it so often? What purpose does it serve? If you are on a path to enlightenment, whether you are studying the Law of Attraction, the teachings of Christ, Buddhist meditation or whatever, ask yourself: *What am I really trying to accomplish here? Why am I on the path?*

As discussed in the "Are We There Yet" section at the end of Part Two, most of us are operating under the assumption (perhaps unconscious) that if we can just get it all figured out—that is, once we learn enough, know enough, behave the right or spiritual or enlightened way all the time—then we can avoid pain altogether.

However, when avoiding pain becomes a primary goal, it limits your emotional repertoire. Eventually you carve out a well-worn path between anger, free-floating anxiety and numbness. When you live this way for long enough, joy becomes an inchoate longing, never to be touched upon because it is too tangled up with emotions you've been avoiding.

I am intimate with the hyper-vigilant attitude that squeezes joy out of life because I used to wear it like a coat of armor. I thought it would protect me from being hurt. It was a survival tool I adopted as a child, and it took many heart-searing experiences to destroy the illusion that I could transcend the natural pain that comes with being alive. The reality that I could not insulate myself from loss was a tough teacher, leading me at some points to despair. I consider it a gift of Grace that at each of those pivotal moments there were people who helped me begin to learn that if I would sit with my pain, neither wallowing in it or trying to push it away, I could tear down the walls around my heart that had left me numb. And when I unwrapped the pain, I found Joy, pulsing and precious, in the fragile center of my Self.

Your ego is totally invested in pain avoidance. When your ego encounters something it doesn't like, it says, *I must be doing something wrong! Otherwise this wouldn't be happening to me! If I can just figure out what I'm doing wrong, I can change it.* Or, *If it's not me, then there's something or someone else at fault. If I can just take control of the situation then I won't hurt anymore.*

You see, at its essence resistance is a judgment that pain is bad.

Human beings create most of their own suffering by resisting pain.

Conscious manifestation is not about helping your ego avoid pain. It is about opening up to WHATEVER is happening in your life right now and trusting that, whatever it is, somewhere in there is a gift for you. It doesn't mean it's what your ego wants. It doesn't mean it doesn't hurt like hell. You don't even have to like it. But if you can bring yourself to stop resisting, if you can say, *It is what it is,* then you create space. And in that space, CONSCIOUS manifestation becomes possible.

EXERCISE:

Begin a practice of noticing resistance in yourself. It may show up as physical discomfort or feelings of being stuck, depressed or helpless. Or a judgment that something in your life is different than it should be. Just notice. And please, don't beat yourself up for resisting. It's what we do.

Now you are noticing the resistance, and that's great. Just give thanks for the awareness.

Make some notes about where you find the most resistance (hint: look for resentments, frustrations, any type of emotional or even physical pain).

Do you notice resistance in some of your relationships?

Do you notice any resistance patterns — situations that almost always produce tension, frustration, fear, irritation or anger?

Where in your body do you typically notice discomfort associated with resistance? (Throat, heart and stomach are common but everyone is unique; for instance, how do you usually get sick?)

Are you open to the idea that your resistance is keeping you from exploring possibilities that would lead you to your heart's deepest longings?

Limiting Attitude #2: Judgment

Judgment is really just another form of resistance to what is. When you judge, you are making up a story. It's a defensive response to something your ego is not pleased about.

We all struggle with judgment at times, and it can take many forms. Take a look at the judgments you make throughout your day. If you are observant, you will realize that your mind generates stories, based on judgments, about virtually every encounter you have. For instance, if someone cuts you off on the highway, where does your mind go? When your partner, child or business colleague is less than pleasant, what do you do with that? When you read an article in the newspaper, what judgments do you make about the people involved? Or about the person writing the story?

Of course, in order to function in life, you will necessarily make some judgments. The key is to notice when you are making them and then get conscious about whether those judgments are giving rise to stories that serve you. Once you are aware of judgment, you can decide moment to moment whether you want to keep the story your mind has offered, make up a new one, or even be in a state of uncertainty where you are letting go of stories altogether.

I'll give you an example of how judgment has operated in my own life.

I've mentioned that our daughter Bridget had several open-heart surgeries (four of them before she was six years old). As you might imagine, I encountered some resistance inside myself around her less-than-perfect condition. Every time she had a cardiac ultrasound scheduled, I would dread the appointment for weeks. And when her doctor gave us the news that she'd need another surgery, I was devastated.

Once in awhile, when I could step outside my emotional turmoil to observe myself, I was fascinated (and occasionally embarrassed) to see the judgments my mind would generate. I had thoughts like: "God is punishing me," or "I must have done something wrong." I told myself, "No mother should ever have to face the possibility that her child will die," and "I can't handle this." I rode an emotional roller coaster. Sometimes I was jealous of people whose children were healthy. Other times I looked for ways to convince myself that the things I saw happening to other children in the hospital (heart transplants, cancer, paralysis from surgery, seizures, death on the operating table or in the intensive care unit) would never happen to Bridget. I had always prided myself on being compassionate, and then I'd be amazed to see myself get irritated with mothers who were dealing with more minor things like ear tubes or broken arms or glasses when I was waiting through eight-hour surgeries with our child on a heart-lung bypass machine.

My thoughts were all variations on a theme, and the theme was: our daughter's heart problems shouldn't be happening.

Obviously, this judgment (though understandable) did not serve me well. I had to make a decision, over and over, to let go of that judgment. Releasing the judgment allowed me to create new stories that empowered me to make the best choices for myself and our daughter.

EXERCISE:

Whenever your mind is trapped in judgment, you'll notice a constant stream of thoughts that clutter your mind and get in the way of conscious manifestation.

Continue observing your thoughts and reactions. When you find yourself annoyed, angry, frustrated, ask: *What assumptions/beliefs/thoughts/stories are giving rise to these feelings?* Curiosity is a place of possibility. To each thought/story/judgment, try saying, *It is what it is.* When another story arises, repeat, *It is what it is.*

See if you are willing to consider letting go of the stories. If you can make this a practice, it will catapult you forward as a conscious manifester. You might make up a new story that serves you better eventually, or even in a few minutes. But be willing to let go of that story, too, when the time is right. That way, you are always living in a place of possibility and choice.

Your Inner Witness: a/k/a The Judgment Dissolver

Once you begin witnessing what your mind is doing, you can begin to ask yourself some interesting questions like: *If I am observing these thoughts, then who is having the thoughts?* Or, *I wonder what purpose this storyline serves?* This line of questioning can pull you right out of your ego gymnastics into a place where you stop identifying so much with your mind. You realize that you are not your thoughts. You are that which lives in the space between thoughts, The Great Space.

Now you are getting somewhere!

Now you have access to the Unified Field, the Otherworld, The Great Space, The Cornucopia Reality. It's here that you meet Essence. This is the place where you consciously begin to create your own reality.

I have learned over the years to step into the Cornucopia Reality at will.

There are many ways to do this, but as discussed earlier, the most efficient way I know is to train your mind through the discipline of meditation. You also access Essence as you apply the steps of The Cornucopia Method of Manifestation. And you have the shortcut advantage of The Manifestation Matrix Meditation to raise your vibrational frequency and make it easier to step into the Cornucopia Reality whenever you want to do it. So keep up the good work! You're developing your inner witness and you're on the superhighway to conscious manifestation.

Limiting Attitude #3: Guilt & Blame

You've probably heard someone (maybe yourself) explain that she (or he) can't have the life she wants because an adverse event (job loss, death of a loved one, end of a relationship, health challenge, etc.) has taken away her ability to experience joy, peace, abundance. But success and happiness are not in fact determined by the events of life. The amount of success and happiness you experience depends on how you respond.

When our daughter Maddie was young, my Dad used to look for opportunities to teach her this lesson. If Maddie became upset because a soccer referee made a "bad" call during one of her games, or she had a conflict with kids at school, he would say, "Maddie, you get to decide exactly how happy you are going to be. The quality of your life has nothing to do with what happens to you. It's how you react to what happens." Since Maddie watched my Dad suffer a heart attack, lose a leg, endure thirty hospitalizations in two years and undergo kidney dialysis three times a week — with equanimity and good humor — his words made a lasting impression on her (and, of course, on me as well). I thought about my Dad's wisdom when I read about

Dr. Paul Stolz, who coined the term Adversity Quotient (AQ) to measure how people respond to perceived setbacks in life. Dr. Stolz's work details the elements that allow people to have a resilient response to adversity, or high AQ. In my work with individuals, I have found that people with a high AQ have four characteristics:

1. They don't blame themselves for setbacks (guilt);
2. They don't blame others (blame);
3. They view all problems as limited in size and duration (manageability) and
4. They perceive themselves as having the capacity to do something constructive in response to their problems (resourcefulness).

EXERCISE: EVALUATE YOUR CURRENT PERSONAL ADVERSITY QUOTIENT

Take a few minutes to evaluate your AQ. Be honest with yourself—just about everyone can improve in this area. The clearer you are about your current AQ, the easier it will be for you to improve it.

Here's my process for evaluating your AQ: Think about a recent situation when you were faced with a challenge. Consider a minor annoyance, something like: you're running late to an appointment. Someone takes your parking spot. You have to deal with an irritating but harmless acquaintance. Or you're watching the playback of your favorite show and the DVR gives you the message: "Due to technical difficulties, some of the recording was lost."

Do you have a scenario in mind from your own life? When you do, on a scale of 1-10, with 1 being the most seriously challenged and 10 being the epitome of grace and ease, rate yourself on these statements:

○ **Guilt/Responsibility Scale:** At the time of the event, I took responsibility for any part I may have played in contributing to the situation without beating myself up (1 = completely false, 10 = absolutely true);

○ **Blame/Forgiveness Scale:** At the time of the event, I was able to accurately assess how others may have contributed to the situation while accepting that most people do the best they can with the resources and information they have at any given moment.

○ **Catastrophization/Managability Scale:** At the time of the event I perceived the challenge as limited in size and duration.

○ **Helplessness/Resourcefulness Scale:** At the time of the event, I perceived myself as having the capacity to do something constructive in response to the situation.

Give yourself a number from 1-10 for each of the four scales (remember, 1 = completely false and 10 = absolutely true).

MY AQ SCORE FOR MINOR ANNOYANCE SITUATIONS IS: _____
(scores can range from 4 to 40)

If your score is 32 or higher, your AQ is well developed for minor annoyances. If your score was lower, congratulations! You've taken the first step in raising your AQ by becoming aware that it is currently lower than optimal for minor annoyance situations.

If your score was anything less than 40 (and if it was 40, were you being completely honest? I'm not suggesting that NO ONE scores a 40 in minor situations, just want to be sure you're getting the most out of the exercise...) then let's do an experiment.

Look at the situation again. With hindsight and your newfound knowledge of the AQ, can you perceive the situation differently? Often it's easier to accurately assess an experience when you aren't in the middle of it. If you can reflect on what happened with more detachment now, then you will likely be less reactive next time you are confronted with a similar situation. If you are unable to see the situation in a different light, that's okay. Go ahead and finish the discussion of the four major obstacles to conscious manifestation and then revisit this exercise later.

Now repeat the exercise for a more moderate stress situation. Think of an actual event you've recently experienced: having a flight cancelled that caused you to miss a connection and an important business meeting, a fairly heated disagreement with someone significant in your life, someone at work blaming you for a problem you didn't create or taking credit for your own contribution. Have a situation in mind? Go back to the four scales for AQ and evaluate yourself again. Add up the four scores.

MY AQ SCORE FOR MODERATELY STRESSFUL SITUATIONS IS: _____

If you were able to raise your score for the minor annoyance situation after you reflected on it, then try that exercise now for the moderately stressful situation. With the buffer of time and your knowledge of the AQ, does your perception of the situation shift at all?

Now let's consider a high stress situation: finding out that a loved one has betrayed you, divorce or separation, death of an intimate relation or some other situation with the potential for a lot of emotional upheaval. Use the four scales to assess your AQ score for high stress.

MY HIGH STRESS AQ SCORE IS: _____

Finally, if you've ever dealt with an ongoing high-stress situation such as being a caregiver for someone who is chronically or terminally ill, long-standing grief following a death of a loved one, or dealing with your own unremitting pain or illness, you may wish to do the AQ exercise again for chronic stress. Ongoing pressure can be debilitating, especially without sufficient support.

MY CHRONIC STRESS AQ SCORE IS: _____

If you are currently in a high or chronic stress situation or still suffering the residual effects, please get the support you need. Seek help. Bodywork, therapy, spiritual direction, support groups and spending time in nature are just a few of the ways you can begin to heal. If you are in this state, set an intention to manifest the perfect sources of support for your individual needs and the resources to have access to them.

Now compare your four AQ scores. Are there significant differences or did your score stay fairly consistent throughout the four evaluations? You might expect everyone to have his (or her) score go down as the level of stress increases. While this is often true, some people actually deal better with real crises than they do with minor annoyances. The only important factor in this exercise is for you to assess yourself as accurately as possible.

If your score was lower than you would like it to be (and almost everyone has room for improvement) then I have some good news for you: AQ can be learned!

The first step in improving your AQ is self-awareness. Read the four positive evaluative AQ statements on page 169 for the scales of guilt/responsibility, blame/forgiveness, catastrophization/manageability and helplessness/resourcefulness each day for several weeks. You might even want to put them on your refrigerator or on your bathroom mirror. As you bring your attention more and more to the qualities of responsibility, forgiveness, manageability and resourcefulness, you will find those qualities present in yourself to a greater degree.

Read on to find out more about how to recognize when you have allowed yourself to become absorbed in guilt and blame so you can interrupt those patterns.

Recognizing the Voice of Guilt

Guilt and blame are really just two types of blame: self-blame (guilt) and blaming others. As we saw in our exploration of the Adversity Quotient (AQ), guilt and blame drain your resilience and block energy you could otherwise be using to focus on what you want.

Guilt is the voice that says to you: *This happened because I'm a terrible person/stupid/mean/a bad parent, child, spouse, friend,* etc. The label may change, but guilt will always offer you some variation on the message: *My life isn't working because there's something wrong with me.* Guess what? When you send out that vibration, life will provide you with plenty of opportunities and evidence to support it.

Guilt may also tell you: *It's not ok for me to be happy/want more/be safe/be at peace/have abundance as long as anyone else is unhappy/experiencing less/in a war zone/anxious/starving...* Do you really want to wait until every being on the planet is consciously manifesting life the way YOU think it should be before you will choose to be happy? Feeling guilty because you have resources that others don't have makes no more sense than rejecting a chance at love because there are some people who aren't in good relationships. Or making detrimental lifestyle choices because some people don't take good care of their bodies.

Guilt does not serve to bring you closer to your dreams. It doesn't help anyone else. And it's not effective in changing behavior. In fact, indulging in guilt is a subtle and seductive trap that allows you to avoid taking charge of your life.

Blame Robs You of Your Power

Like guilt, blame is a trap, in part because it is so easy to blame another person or situation for what isn't working in your life. Blame may be easy, but it is also soul-depleting.

If you are human, then I know you've been hurt. I know other people have let you down, betrayed you and lied to you. You experience disappointments. You may even have suffered abuse or torture. I don't wish to minimize your experience.

Yet whether your pain is large or small, I challenge you to look at how blame constricts your energy. As long as someone or something else is to blame for what you perceive to be current problems, then you are stuck. You are disempowered. You'll always be looking to someone else to change their behavior, or waiting to be punished or rewarded by life, fate, luck or God.

But perhaps you are wondering, if you don't look outside of yourself to determine who's at fault for the painful circumstances of your life, are you then forced to resort back to guilt? After all, isn't *someone* to blame? Guilt and blame are two sides of the same coin. Imagine these attitudes as balls of dense, dark energy. Most of us spend our lives passing these balls back and forth.

Where did the dense energies come from?

At some point in the evolution of our species, human beings came to the conclusion that emotional pain, instead of being a gift that leads us to self-knowledge and expansion, was a curse. Call it original sin or original resistance, this is the idea that if something feels uncomfortable, we need to run away from it, punish ourselves for feeling it, or direct it at someone else. We bought into the lie that things aren't the way they're supposed to be (remember judgment?) and therefore someone must be to blame. If it's not me, it's you. If it's not you, then it's him. Or her. Or them. Or it. Like some crazy cosmic game of hot potato.

173

As long as we keep throwing this dense energy at each other or carrying it around in our own bodies, we are trapped in old ways of thinking and behaving that keep us small. We are cut off from ourselves and each other. Our individual pockets of dense energies coalesce and become monstrous, unconscious entities that lead us to fight individually and en masse about everything from territory to money to religion.

Freedom from this madness lies in the ability to re-connect to your Essential Self and the Source of who you are. In doing so, you will find the space and strength to re-integrate your own small part of the collective shadow material. And you will have stepped out of the guilt/blame game.

How does this process of healing happen? It begins with true responsibility.

True Response-ability

As I've mentioned before, one of the biggest forms of resistance is resistance to accepting complete responsibility for your life — acknowledging that whatever is happening right now is a perfect mirror of the energetic projections you've been sending out to the Universe. Most of those projections have happened outside of your conscious awareness; however, even if you don't understand HOW you manifested your current reality, you can still begin to change it right now...by accepting that responsibility.

Blame, whether it's focused on yourself as guilt or on something outside of you (the economy, your partner/child/parent/boss/friend, the circumstances of your birth, the weather...you name it), is a way of avoiding true responsibility. Blame and guilt paralyze you. As long as your energy is focused on berating yourself or blaming someone or something else, you are powerless to change your situation.

True responsibility is the answer, and this is what it looks like: First, you recognize there is something in your life you'd like to change. You may be aware of what it is, or you might just recognize a feeling of dis-ease, frustration, restlessness or discomfort. You give thanks for that awareness. You immediately move to access a state of compassion via meditation (or whatever method you use for remembering your connection to Essence).

Whether or not you experience the profound state of existential Grace that lives in the Unified Field, you act as if it is there. You offer Grace and Compassion to yourself. Bathed in compassion, you feel safe enough to be honest about how your level of consciousness, thoughts, beliefs, emotions, feelings and behaviors have contributed to your present state of being. You can assess your situation accurately, dispassionately and without judgment. You can determine whether and how you've harmed yourself and/or others and make amends where appropriate. And you are empowered to move forward and create something new.

Do you remember the four measurements of AQ (Adversity Quotient)? People with high resiliency or AQ:

o   Don't blame themselves
o   Don't blame others
o   View all problems as limited in size and duration
o   View themselves as capable of doing something constructive to address any situation

Responsibility is response-ability. It allows you to take constructive action in any situation.

Sometimes response-ability is the decision to adopt an attitude of peace in the midst of chaos. To offer yourself compassion. To tend to your anger, despair, frustration and fear instead of allowing them to act for you. Sometimes responsibility is realizing after the fact that you acted while in the grips of a challenging emotion and now you need to honestly address the consequences without guilt or blame.

First and foremost, response-ability is Presence. It's bringing your whole self to the moment.

Don't expect guilt and blame to disappear entirely from your life. They may pop up with some regularity. But now you will recognize them for what they are: distractions that trick you into forgetting your awesome co-creative power.

Limiting Attitude #4: Pretending

The fourth and final common obstacle to conscious manifestation is Pretending.

You may be confused by this statement if you've read other materials on manifestation because you've probably heard that if you want to manifest something, you need to act as if you already have it, and that is true.

However, there's a subtle and critical difference between "acting as if," which is an important element of manifestation, and pretending, which impedes the realization of your dreams.

"Acting as if" means putting yourself in the mindset and emotional experience that you'd be having if you were where you wanted to be, having what you wanted to have. Then you ACT as if you already were the person who would be having those experiences. When you are authentically "acting as if," you are consistently hanging out in the vibration of what you desire and your behaviors flow out of that vibration. When that happens, what you want (or something that has a matching vibrational frequency) will naturally come to you. According to the Law of Attraction, this can and must happen.

"Acting as if" means becoming the person you would be, having the inner experience you would have if you had already realized your manifestation goal.

This does NOT mean you pretend things are different than they are. You just let go of the stories you've been making up about the way things are, and that frees you to experience your inner joy. When you are in Joy, your actions are different than when you are in lack. You become a different person.

In contrast, pretending is a form of denial. It goes beyond releasing your storylines to putting your head in the sand about the way things are. This is disempowering, and because your unconscious is still aware of the facts you're avoiding on some level, you are carrying the vibrations of worry, anxiety, fear, etc., in your field. And then that's what you attract.

What Pretending Looks Like

Joyce, a woman in her fifties, begins having some distressing physical symptoms, including gastrointestinal discomfort and lack of energy. At first she dismisses the experience as a virus or something she ate. A few days go by. Symptoms continue and intensify. Days turn into weeks. Her pallor becomes pale, then takes on a grayish tinge. Her belly begins to swell. She becomes so weak she can't walk well anymore. She sends her husband to the drugstore to pick up a cane, she cuts down on her activities and quits going out of the house. But she does not go to the doctor. When friends and family express concern, she dismisses their questions. A few months later, she collapses and dies. At the hospital the doctors tell her husband that her heart gave out and that her body was riddled with cancer.

That's pretending. Joyce ignored the signals her body was giving her that something was amiss. Perhaps she suspected the truth, but instead of facing it and making a conscious choice about how to address her illness and her mortality (which, let's face it, is an issue for all of us whether we have cancer or not), she pretended. And in doing so, she failed to show up for the moment. She missed the opportunities for healing on physical, relational and spiritual levels that would have come with bringing her full presence to life's messiness.

In contrast, "acting as if" would look something like this: Joyce notices her symptoms. She takes it easy for a few days, but in spite of getting extra rest and eating lightly, her symptoms intensify. She makes an appointment to see a doctor. Tests reveal cancer. She is terrified and yet she moves fairly quickly into a more neutral assessment of her situation and what can be done. She does research about her treatment options.

She notices her fears as they arise. Occasionally she is swallowed up by them. She rails at God and screams in the shower. And...she keeps coming back to her breath. She awakens to the wonder of her existence. She begins to ponder what death will be like, whether it arrives sooner or later, whether it comes wearing the face of cancer or some other mask.

She finds new meaning in her relationships and even in this body that seems to have failed her. She reaches out for support and makes the changes in her life necessary to give almost all of her attention and energy to spiritual, physical, mental and emotional healing. Each day she gives thanks for her body's resilience and for its brilliance in letting her know that it needed attending to. She says to herself things like: *I am an expression of the creative healing power of God. My body's ability to heal is as great as the Universe itself.*

She looks for the humor in the absurdities of life. She laughs. She gathers with family and friends when she has the energy. She is gentle with herself. And when she forgets to be gentle with herself, she forgives herself for that. She cries when she feels like crying. She gives herself what she needs. She acts as if she is alive, because she is. And she acts as if this is the most important moment in her life. Because it is.

EXERCISE:
Think of a situation in your own life where you resorted to denial or pretending. What happened? Are you pretending about anything right now?

Now consider whether there is any area of your life that would benefit from an exercise in "acting as if." If you want more money, for instance, what can you do to put yourself in the feeling state you'd be experiencing, if you had all the resources you need in this moment? *(Hint: you DO have everything you need).* Can you access a state of abundance you feel in some area other than money (e.g. health, relationships, intellectual stimulation) and allow that feeling to grow until it colors how you feel about your financial situation as well?

If you want a different home, or relationship, or career, or car, or life, ask yourself: *Who would I have to become to bring that experience into my reality? And how would that person act right here, right now, in my current situation? Where would I be putting my time and energy? What would I be reading? Where would I be going? What would I be doing?* Once you have the answers to those questions, begin acting as if you are that person who has the life you want. When you become the person who has that life, that life will show up for you.

The Divine Marriage

As you notice — and then release — the very human reactions of resistance, judgment, guilt/blame and pretending, something magical happens. You start to act as if your life is a gift. You remember who you are: an expression of Essence. You enter into an ecstatic, co-creative dance with the Divine. You begin to express yourself as the magnificent being you are.

Before we complete this part of our journey together, I'll share an ancient story that hints at your true nature: the myth of Psyche and Cupid.

Once upon a time, in the country of Greece, there lived a maiden named Psyche.

Psyche's face, form and way of being were lovely to behold. She was so universally loved and admired, in fact, that people stopped bringing offerings to Aphrodite, the goddess of love. Instead, they wrote poems and stories about Psyche. Aphrodite became jealous and angry. She summoned her son Cupid.

"Cupid, I grow tired of hearing about this maiden, Psyche. Songs of her beauty are spreading across the lands and over the seas. Even the gods are admiring her! Go to her. Pierce her with one of your love arrows. But not just any arrow. Enchant her so that she becomes enamored with a monster!"

Cupid flew in through Psyche's window that night as she slept. He felt a pang of regret as he pulled the special arrow out if his quiver. Surely, he ought not to corrupt such loveliness? What good could come of forcing a woman – any woman – to pine after a monster?

Suddenly, Psyche awoke. She looked directly into Cupid's eyes, even though he should have been invisible to her. Startled, Cupid accidentally pricked himself with the arrow and fell hopelessly in love. Confused and overwhelmed by his own emotions, Cupid fled.

Meanwhile, Psyche's mother and father became confused and concerned about their daughter's lack of suitors. Psyche had many admirers, but they were all too awed by her to consider her as a mate. So Psyche's parents traveled to Delphi to seek the advice of Apollo's oracle.

At Delphi, Cupid directed the oracle to say that Psyche's beauty made her unsuitable for a mortal spouse. Psyche's parents were devastated but resigned to the oracle's word. They dressed Psyche in bridal clothes and then walked with her to a desolate mountainside, where they left her alone to meet the will of the gods.

After her parents had gone, a gentle wind arose and carried Psyche to a lavish palace. Servants attended to her every need. And that night, in the dark, she met her new husband.

Psyche sensed that her husband was immortal. After all, hadn't the oracle told her she would not marry a human man? Her spouse came to her each night. He was tender and loving with her, but cautioned her never to light a lamp or seek to look at him.

After a time, Psyche became lonely for her home and family, so she invited her sisters to visit. When Psyche's sisters arrived, they admired her magnificent home and listened to her descriptions of her attentive husband. But when she admitted she had never seen him, the sisters became suspicious. Why would he not show himself? They insisted that no worthy husband would have need to mask his true identity. What if she had married a monster?

Psyche was torn and confused. She believed herself in love, but her sisters' questions deepened her disquiet about never knowing her husband by day. What was he hiding, after all?

That night, when her husband fell asleep, Psyche lit a candle. As the warm glow illuminated her beloved's sleeping form, Psyche realized he was not a monster, but Cupid, the beautiful being she had seen once in a dream. Just as she realized her husband's true nature, Psyche spilled a drop of wax on his chest, and he awoke.

Realizing that Psyche now knew his identity, Cupid fled. He did not believe that Aphrodite would ever allow them to remain together.

Bereft, Psyche wandered the land, seeking her husband, but he was nowhere to be found. Eventually, heedless of Aphrodite's anger, Psyche went to the goddess's temple and begged her to reunite them.

Aphrodite heard Psyche's pleas. "I will bring you to Cupid. But first, you must show me you are worthy of my son." So, she ordered Psyche to complete several dangerous, impossible tasks.

But the other gods were not oblivious to Psyche's plight. Impressed by her determination and great love, several of the Olympians came to her aid and allowed her to triumph.

Ultimately, Zeus himself, ruler of the Olympians, asked Aphrodite to give her blessing to Psyche and Cupid's marriage. Psyche drank the Ambrosia of the gods, which rendered her immortal.

And of course, you know the rest.

They lived happily ever after.

Why should you care about a story from ancient Greece?

Because, no matter where you live, or when, it is your story too. It is the story of forgetting, and remembering, who you are.

Psyche is your soul. A soul that wears a human disguise for this sojourn on earth. A soul that forgets its immortality in its eagerness to immerse itself in the space-time continuum.

Throughout its travels, your soul will get reminders of its true nature. They will come disguised as disappointments, failures and tragedies. They will whisper to you in a sense of vague dissatisfaction, even in the midst of your successes. A sense that, *There must be more to life than this.* (Because there is).

Every joyful experience, every difficult moment, every seemingly impossible task, holds a door open for your soul. It is a viewscreen into your true nature. A portal to your immortality. A reminder of the Divine Marriage.

There is nowhere else to go. No one else for you to be. Everything you need is right here. Right now. All you need do is open your eyes, your heart and your mind. See you on Olympus.

Advice for Psyche

Stay away from
solutions, my friend.
Stop trying to feel
better.

Your discontent
is calling you
to your greatness.

Ignore it at your peril.

Those little rituals
you do to ease your daily dread
only postpone
the inevitable.

Why avoid the reckoning?

What makes you want to run
from the ravishment
of your soul?

Are you really that enamored
with pretending to be less
than you are?

Here is the truth now:
(you might want to sit down for this).

You are never
going to die.

You are a Cosmic Creator
masquerading as
a creation.

And all these dress rehearsals
for your illusory demise,
these lavish lacerations
of your carefully crafted ego...

are invitations
to step into
your eternality.

183

Quit playing by the rules
of engagement
and just be engaged.

Eschew whatever soothes
the terror you won't name.

Sit down instead,
right next to your fear.
Let it stoke your holy longing
for something
this world
can never
satisfy.

Laugh at your failures.

Delight in your petty
humiliations.

These are the doorways
to your coronation
on Olympus.

Remember
Remember
Remember
Who You Are.

The Divine Marriage
has always been yours
for the asking.

©2009 Kimberly V. Schneider

Where Do You Go from Here?

You've finished reading *Everything You Need Is Right Here*. Perhaps you've worked through the exercises and kept a journal to record your observations and track your changes. So what will you do with what you've learned? My first suggestion would be to read the book again. Do the exercises again. And again. Better yet, start an *Everything*

You Need Is Right Here book group. When you read something once and don't do anything else with it, you lose 85% of the information within fifteen days. But if you expose yourself to that information at least twenty times over a thirty-day period — in many different ways — you will retain 85% of the concepts. More importantly, the new information will begin to impact the way you think, feel and behave. *And when that happens, your life changes.*

So repetition is absolutely necessary. Think about it: if you want to undo a lifetime of Unconscious Limiting Beliefs and replace them with something that works better for you, it will take more than a one- time read-through of this book. However, if you've done the exercises and begun to integrate the five steps of The Cornucopia Method of Manifestation, then you are already changing. And the more ways you can find to integrate this information into your life, the more quickly and more deeply those ideas will take root.

I hope to see you at one of my events or at a sacred site workshop in western Ireland or Europe, or perhaps connect with you via an individual session. There's also a resource guide at the back of the book to assist you in furthering your studies. My sincere wish and hope is that I've played some part in expanding your consciousness and enhancing your life with this book.

My passion is to help create as many conscious manifesters on this planet as I can. Thanks for being part of my dream. You are here to create magic and miracles, here and now. Make it so.

Abundant Blessings,

TheManifestationMaven.com

Part Four

Resources

Resources for Further Learning and Expansion

First, a caveat. This list is completely arbitrary.

I'm aware as I'm compiling it that I might be leaving out some amazing resource, some book or audio program or website that helped me and would also be wonderful for you. I've drawn upon a lifetime of learning and experience to create the material in this book, including what probably amounts to several thousand books, CD programs, DVDs and seminars. I may have forgotten something. Nevertheless, these are definitely some of my favorites. I also have a resource website, **FindsForSeekers.com**, from which you can order books, CDs and DVDs right from Amazon. Most of the items listed here can also be found there. In a couple clicks you can find my recommendations in different categories and then have a particular item sent right to your house. I add new items to the site from time to time, so it may be more up to date than this list.

Five other resources I'd like to mention especially:

- **My free e-Course on Manifestation**, available at **TheManifestationMaven.com**, will provide you with some nice reminders of the concepts in this book. Additionally, when you request the e-Course I'll be sure to send you periodic manifestation and consciousness tips. I'll also let you know about events I'm offering and new resources I've encountered that I'm happy to pass on to you. (Incidentally, if you've downloaded one of the free audios I made for you, you should already have received the free e-Course as well. Please email me at **support@KimberlySchneider.com** if you did not get it).

- **The Dancing on the Edge: A Celtic Soul Experience workshop** I facilitate in western Ireland. This Celtic Soul Experience in western Ireland is not just a tour of sites. It is a spiritual journey, a weeklong transformational workshop and enlivening retreat. While you won't see all or even most of Ireland, you will touch its soul. Or perhaps it is more accurate to say that Ireland's soul will open your own soul to something ancient and wild within you. While your soul will be stretched, your capacity for wonder and fun will expand as well. Our journey together moves easily between awe-inspiring treks and toe-tapping music, contemplative moments and laughter over pints of Guinness in the pubs. There will be time for shopping and singing, dancing and drinking, feasting and frolicking, relishing and remembering, walking and wondering... every part of you will be engaged and welcomed. For more information go to: **KimberlySchneider.com/trips.**

- **My manifestation page on Facebook** is a great place to contact me with questions. I visit the page frequently and answer questions personally so be sure to post your thoughts there! The Facebook page is also the first place I post any announcement about new things coming up so it is a wonderful way to stay in touch with what I'm doing. I hope to see you there. **Facebook.com/KimberlyVSchneider** (please note the "v" in the middle of the name there...that's my middle initial and you must include it to get to my FB page).

- Many of the poems reproduced in this book, along with other original poetry, can be found in **my audiobook, Terrible Beauty: Poems and Reflections for Precarious Times**, produced by Avalon Emerging Press. Look for it at **KimberlySchneider.com.**

- **Your free Manifestation Matrix Meditation audio**. If you haven't already downloaded it, you can do that at: **kimberlyschneider.com/manifestationmatrixaudio.** You can download the audio directly to your computer and then put it on an mp3 player or burn it to a CD, whichever is most convenient for you.

Finally, regarding the list of resources below, I created several categories so you can find items that most relate to your areas of interest. Please note that there's a lot of overlap in these categories. Many of the resources could have gone into several places, but I picked the one I thought most appropriate.

Obviously, I love to read and listen and learn. I'm always learning something new or re-working an old idea. But don't ever make the mistake of letting learning be a substitute for living. You can take in all sorts of information, but if you aren't ACTING on it, you're life is never going to change. Before you pick up one more book, ask yourself if you've begun to implement what you learned in this one. If not, go back and find something you can do differently NOW! Then, if you need help understanding a concept or deepening into an idea, look for other resources to help you.

Consciousness & The Nature of Reality

Bradley, Marion Z. *The Mists of Avalon*. New York: Knopf, 1982.

Chopra, Deepak. *Life After Death: the Burden of Proof*. New York: Three Rivers Press, 2008.

Gilbert, Elizabeth. *Eat, Pray, Love: One Woman's Search for Everything Across Italy, India and Indonesia*. New York: Viking, 2006.

Heaven, Ross. *The Sin Eater's Last Confessions: Lost Traditions of Celtic Shamanism*. Woodbury, MN: Llewellyn, 2008.

Jung, Carl G. *Man and His Symbols*. New York: Dell, 1968.

Lipton, Bruce H. *The Biology of Belief: Unleashing the Power of Consciousness, Matter and Miracles.* Carlsbad, CA: Hay House: 2008.

McTaggart, Lynne. *The Intention Experiment: Using Your Thoughts to Change Your Life and the World.* New York: Free Press: 2008.

MacEowen, Frank. *The Mist-Filled Path: Celtic Wisdom for Exiles, Wanderers and Seekers.* Novato, CA: New World Library, 2002.

Rowling, J.K. *Harry Potter Series* (Books I-VII). New York: Arthur A. Levine Books.

Starhawk. *The Fifth Sacred Thing.* New York: Bantam, 1993.

Villoldo, Alberto. *Courageous Dreaming: How Shamans Dream the World into Being.* Carlsbad, CA: Hay House, 2008.

What the Bleep Do We Know? DVD.

Embodiment

Farmer, Angela. *Inner Body Flow* and *The Feminine Unfolding.* DVDs.

Levine, Peter. *Waking the Tiger: Healing Trauma.* Berkley, CA: North Atlantic Books: 1997.

McLaren, Karla. *Rebuilding the Garden: Healing the Wounds of Childhood Sexual Assault.* Columbia, CA: Laughing Tree Press, 1997.

Reeves, Paula M., and Marion Woodman. *Women's Intuition: Unlocking the Wisdom of the Body.* Berkley, CA: Conari Press, 1999.

Roth, Gabrielle. *Sweat Your Prayers*. New York: Tarcher, 1998.

Singh, Ravi and Ana Brett. *Kundalini Yoga for Beginners & Beyond*. DVD. 2005.

Tuholske, Pat. **elementalearthcamp.com** and **willowrainherbalgoods.com** (Herbalist & Shaman)

Emotional & Psychological Awareness

Dweck, Carol. *Mindset: The New Psychology of Success*. New York: Ballantine, 2007.

Hahn, Thich Nhat. *Anger: Wisdom for Cooling the Flames*. New York: Riverhead Trade, 2002.

Riso, Don Richard and Russ Hudson. *The Wisdom of the Enneagram*. New York: Bantam, 1999.

Energetic Awareness & Healing

Eden, Donna. *Energy Medicine: Balancing Your Body's Energies for Optimal Health, Joy and Vitality* and *Energy Medicine for Women: Aligning Your Body's Energies to Boost Your Health and Vitality*. New York: Tarcher, 2008.

Hawkins, David R. *Power vs. Force: the Hidden Determinants of Human Behavior*. Carlsbad, CA: Hay House, 1995.

Myss, Caroline. *Anatomy of Spirit: The Seven Stages of Power and Healing*. New York: Three Rivers Press, 1996.

Orloff, Judith. *Positive Energy: 10 Extraordinary Prescriptions for Transforming Fatigue, Stress, and Fear Into Vibrance, Strength & Love*. New York: Harmony Books, 2004.

Saradananda, Swami. *Chakra Meditation: Discover Energy, Creativity, Focus, Love, Communication, Wisdom, and Spirit.* London: Duncan Baird, 2008.

St. Julian, Samantha. *Synergia Healing Arts.* (2-Volume audio CD set), also available for instant download at **Synergia.bz**. The Synergia website, **Synergia.bz**, is a must-visit for anyone interested in expanding their consciousness or catapulting their healing. Dr. St. Julian is the creator of Synergia and a cutting-edge practitioner in the transformation of our planet. Samantha offers individual healing sessions by phone, Synergia study groups, Synergia trainings in person and online, Synergia CDs and all sorts of unique healing tools. Check her out. After you do, you'll begin to think of your life in terms of Before Samantha and After Samantha. The changes will be that dramatic.

Imagination/Creative Thinking

O'Donohue, John. *Anam Cara: A Book of Celtic Wisdom.* New York: Harper Collins, 1998. Also available in CD/audio format (highly recommended).

Sark. Any of her books!

Whyte, David. *Clear Mind, Wild Heart.* Sounds True: Louisville, CO, Audio CD; *Riverflow: New and Selected Poems.* Langley, WA: Many Rivers Press, 2007; *The Poetry of Self-Compassion.* Audio CD.

Intuition

Choquette, Sonia. *Trust Your Vibes.* Carlsbad, CA: Hay House, 2005.

Emery, Marcia. *Dr. Marcia Emery's Intuition Workbook.* Upper Saddle River, NJ: Prentice Hall, 1994.

Estes, Clarissa Pinkola. *Women Who Run with the Wolves.* New York: Ballantine, 1996.

Naparstek, Bellaruth. *Your Sixth Sense.* New York: Harper One, 2009.

Orloff, Judith. *Dr. Judith Orloff's Guide to Intuitive Healing: 5 Steps to Physical, Emotional and Sexual Wellness.* New York: Three Rivers Press, 2001.

Meditation/Mindfulness

Chodron, Pema. *Awakening Compassion* and *Good Medicine.* Audio CDs. Louisville, CO: Sounds True.

Easwaran, Eknath. *Passage Meditation: Bringing the Deep Wisdom of the Heart into Daily Life; Conquest of Mind; The Mantram Handbook; Take Your Time; Timeless Wisdom: Passages for Meditation from the World's Saints and Sages.* Tomales, CA: Nilgiri Press.

Mingyur, Yongey Rinpoche. *The Joy of Living: Unlocking the Secret of Happiness.* New York: Harmony Books, 2007.

Quinn, Mick. *The Uncommon Path of Awakening Authentic Joy.* UK: O Books, 2009.

Tolle, Eckhart. *A New Earth: Awakening to Your Life's Purpose*. New York: Penguin, 2008, and *The Power of Now: A Guide to Spiritual Enlightenment*. Novato, CA: New World Library, 2004.

Manifestation

Braden, Gregg. *The Lost Mode of Prayer*. Audio CD, and *The Spontaneous Healing of Belief*. Carlsbad, CA: Hay House, 2009.

Byrne, Rhonda. *The Secret*. DVD. If you can find it, I highly recommend the out- of- print version of the DVD that includes Esther and Jerry Hicks. The Hicks's work, frankly, is foundational to the entire premise of the movie, and I feel that the later versions lack the clarity and the depth that the Hicks's work provides.

Chopra, Deepak. *The Spontaneous Fulfillment of Desire: Harnessing the Infinite Power of Coincidence*. New York: Harmony Books, 2003. The audio version of this book is also excellent.

Coelho, Paulo. *The Alchemist*. New York: Harper Collins, 2006.

Dyer, Wayne W. *Meditations for Manifesting: Morning and Evening Meditations to Literally Create Your Heart's Desire*. Audio CD.

Hicks, Esther and Jerry. *The Law of Attraction: The Basics of the Teachings of Abraham*. Carlsbad, CA: Hay House, 2006.

Introducing Abraham: The Secret Behind "The Secret." Exec. Producer Peter Beamish and Producer Annette Repstock. Perf. Esther Hicks, Jerry Hicks, Peter Beamish. Hay House: Carlsbad, CA: Hay House, 2007. DVD.

Maltz, Maxwell. *New Psycho-Cybernetics*. New York: Prentice Hall, 2002.

Shinn, Florence S. *The Wisdom of Florence Scovel Shinn*.

Music

Music is an instant vibration-raising tool. Use it! I have an extensive CD and mp3 collection. Here are a few artists I turn to again and again to touch my soul and raise my spirits:

Byrne, Seamus. *Brother Seamus: The Celtic Spirit* and *The Healer*. To learn more about Brother Seamus' music go to the website at **brotherseamus.ie**

Das, Krishna. *Heart as Wide as the World*. Krishna Das is known all over the world for bringing the practice of Kirtan, the ancient Sanskrit call and repeat practice of chanting sacred phrases, to the masses.

Ni Riain, Noirin. Noirin is an internationally renowned Irish vocalist whose music is uplifting and healing. She consistently brings people to tears with her voice. Anything by Noirin is highly recommended. A couple of my very favorites include *Celtic Soul* and *Celtic Joy*. Noirin recorded the latter work with her sons, Owen and Moley O'Suilleabhain, and the harmonies are exquisite (see below, Size2Shoes, for more on Owen and Moley). I interviewed Noirin for my radio show — check out the recording at WebTalkRadio.net (search my name, Kimberly Schneider, and then look in the archived shows; Noirin's interview is entitled "Direct Line to God.") Any one of Noirin's CDs will transport and heal you. You'll find Noirin's recordings at her website, **Theosony.com**. Noirin is also the author of the book *Listen with the Ear of the Heart*. Dublin: Veritas Publications, 2010. I highly recommend this profoundly spiritual and honest autobiography, which not only tells her own story, but also invites the reader into a more intimate relationship with God.

Premal, Deva. *Dakshina.* Sanskrit chants with cool backbeats and instrumental accompaniment—sort of what Enya would sound like if she had been raised in an Ashram instead of an Irish traditional-music family. Also try *Mantras for Precarious Times*—a wonderful way to calm the mind when life gets turbulent.

Rivera, Faith. *Maluhia.* Danceable, consciousness-infused tunes!

Size2Shoes. Size2Shoes are Owen and Michael ("Moley") O'Suilleabhain, two brothers who've been called "the best singer-songwriters in Ireland." Russell Crowe and Steven Spielberg are big fans of Size2Shoes' "inspirational acoustic pop," which includes upbeat music, sweet harmonies, humor and positive messages. You just can't listen to these guys without feeling good. **Size2Shoes.com**. In fact, I was so inspired when I met Moley and Owen that I hired them to play for the first group I brought to Ireland, and then I produced a week-long series of events in the States for Size2Shoes and Noirin Ni Riain, including a three-city tour and a Celtic Spirituality workshop. Their self-titled debut CD is a refreshing mix that always sounds great to me even after hundreds of plays, and their second CD is due out in 2012.

Wealth Consciousness

Carroll, Lenedra J. *The Architecture of All Abundance: Seven Foundations to Prosperity.* Novato, CA: New World Library, CA, 2003.

Castle, Victoria. *The Trance of Scarcity: Stop Holding Your Breath and Start Living Your Life*. Sagacious Press, 2006.

Chopra, Deepak. *Creating Affluence: The A-to-Z Steps to a Richer Life*. Novato, CA: New World Library, 1998.

Cohen, Alan. *Relax Into Wealth: How to Get More by Doing Less*. New York: Tarcher, 2006.

Hill, Napoleon. *Think and Grow Rich*.

Ponder, Catherine. *Dynamic Laws of Prosperity*. Camarillo, CA: DeVorss & Co., 1962.

Roman, Sanaya, and Duane Packer. *Creating Money: Keys to Abundance*. Tiburon, CA: HJ Kramer, 1988.

Scheinfeld, Robert. *Busting Loose from the Money Game*. Hoboken, NJ: Wiley, 2006.

Shinn, Florence Scovel. ANY of her books. Florence Scovel Shinn was a metaphysical genius and she's my favorite author on wealth consciousness.

Wilde, Stuart. *The Little Money Bible*. Carlsbad, CA: Hay House, 2001.

Please Note: Most of these Resources can be found and ordered through Amazon at findsforseekers.com. Enjoy!

Notes

 *Notes*

Notes

Made in the USA
Charleston, SC
17 February 2012